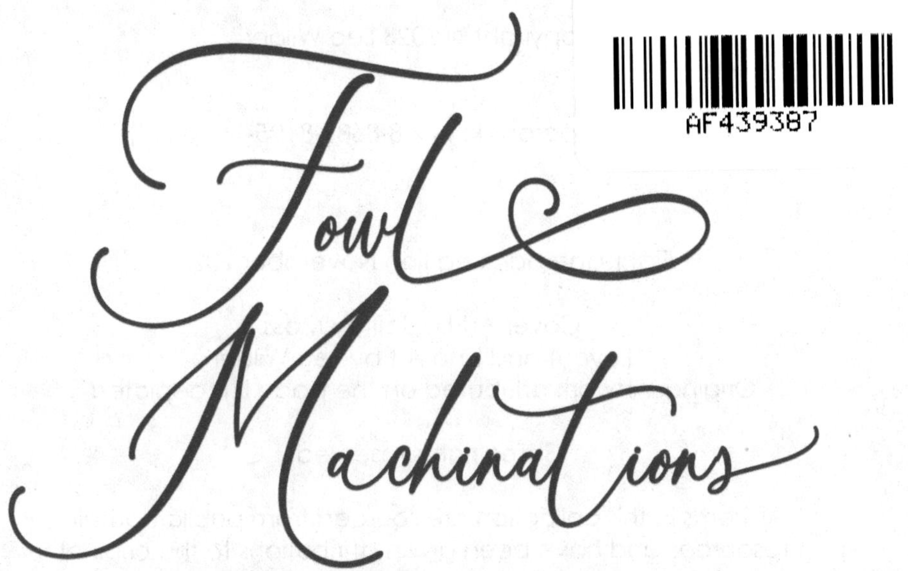

A Collection of Chicken Art
Across the World and Throughout Time

Dedicated to my dear sister
and her chicken army

Paperback: 979-8-8689-8195-1

First paperback edition November 2023.

Cover Art by Jeffrey Moss
Layout and Line Art by Lee Wilder
Original Artwork attributed on the page it is depicted

Printed by Ingram Spark.

Kris & Co. Press
P.O. Box 5102
Mesa, AZ 85211

leewilderbooks.com

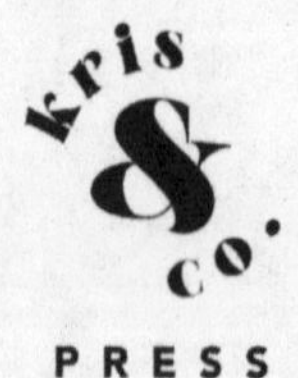

Other works by Lee Wilder

Activity Books
        Egyptian Hieroglyphs: Coloring and Activity Book
        Secrets of Egypt: Journal and Puzzle Book

Children's Picture Books
        Endangered Fairytails Series
                The Ugly Kitten
                Three Little Otters
                Goldiscales and the Three Honey Badgers
                Axolotl

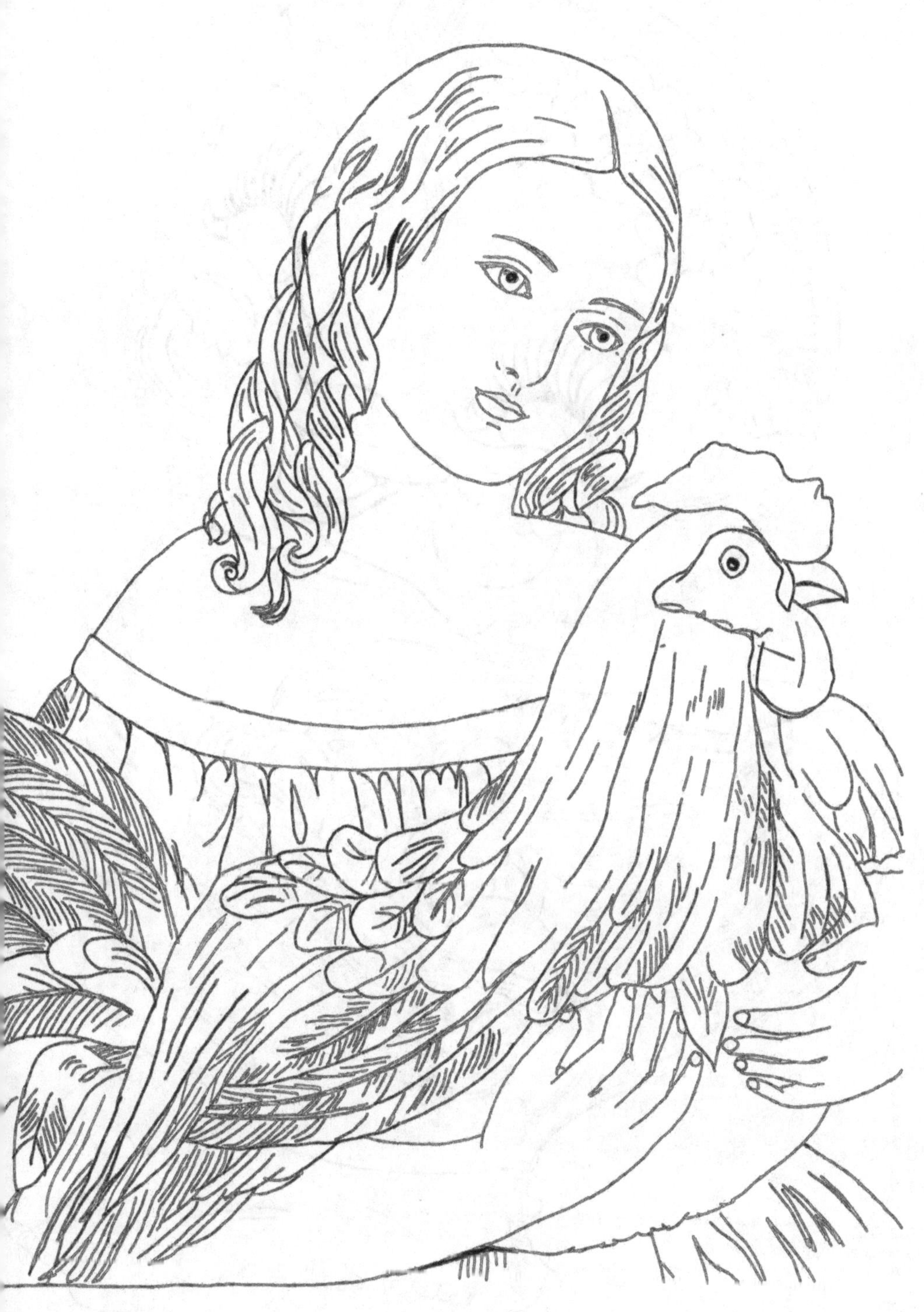

National Museum of American History
Title: The Farmers Pet
Artist: Unknown
Medium: Color Lithograph

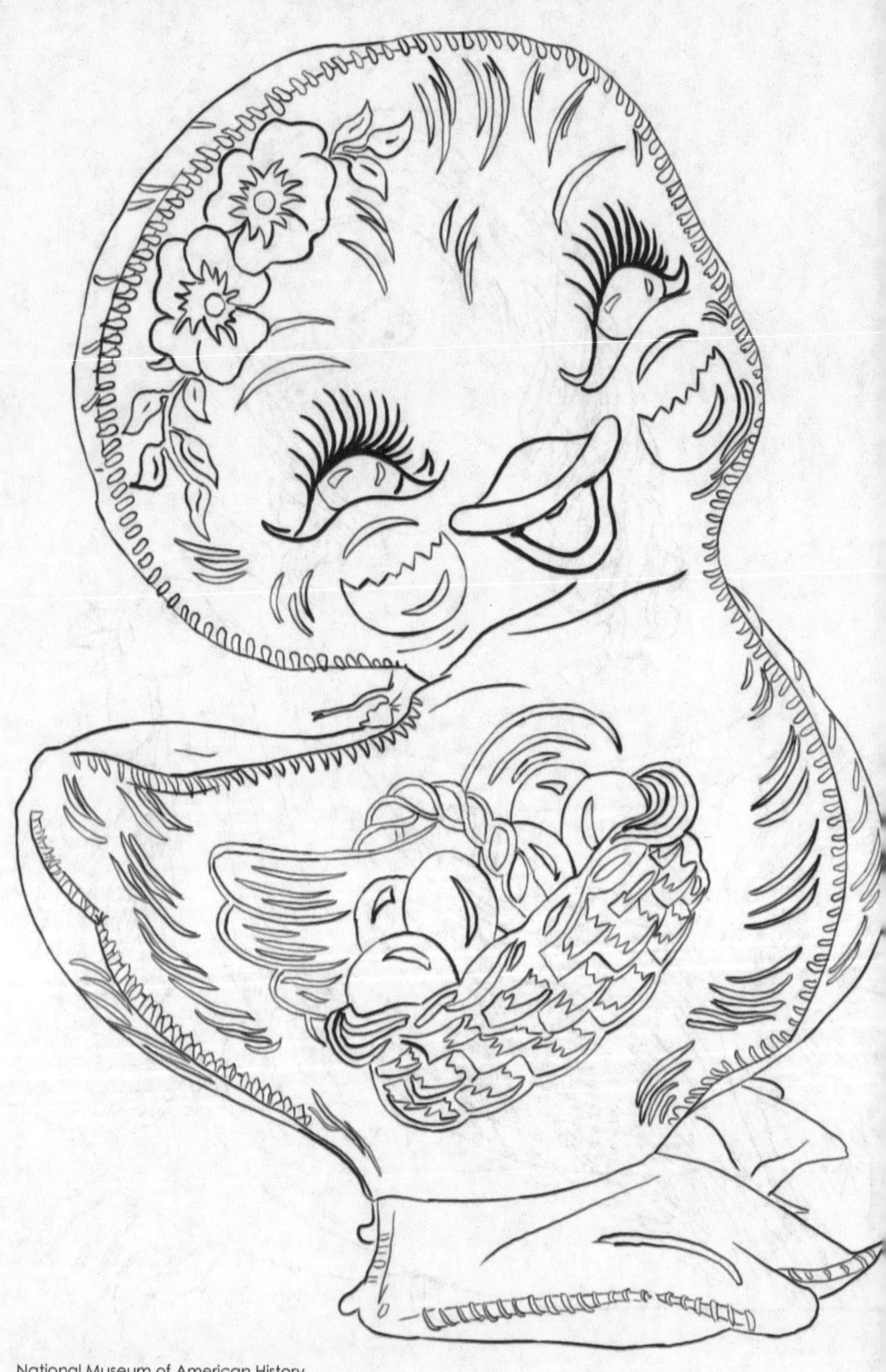

National Museum of American History
Title: Chicken, Stuffed
Artist:Jane Griffin Yeingst and William H. Yeingst
Meduim: Vinyl (overall material), fiber (overall material)

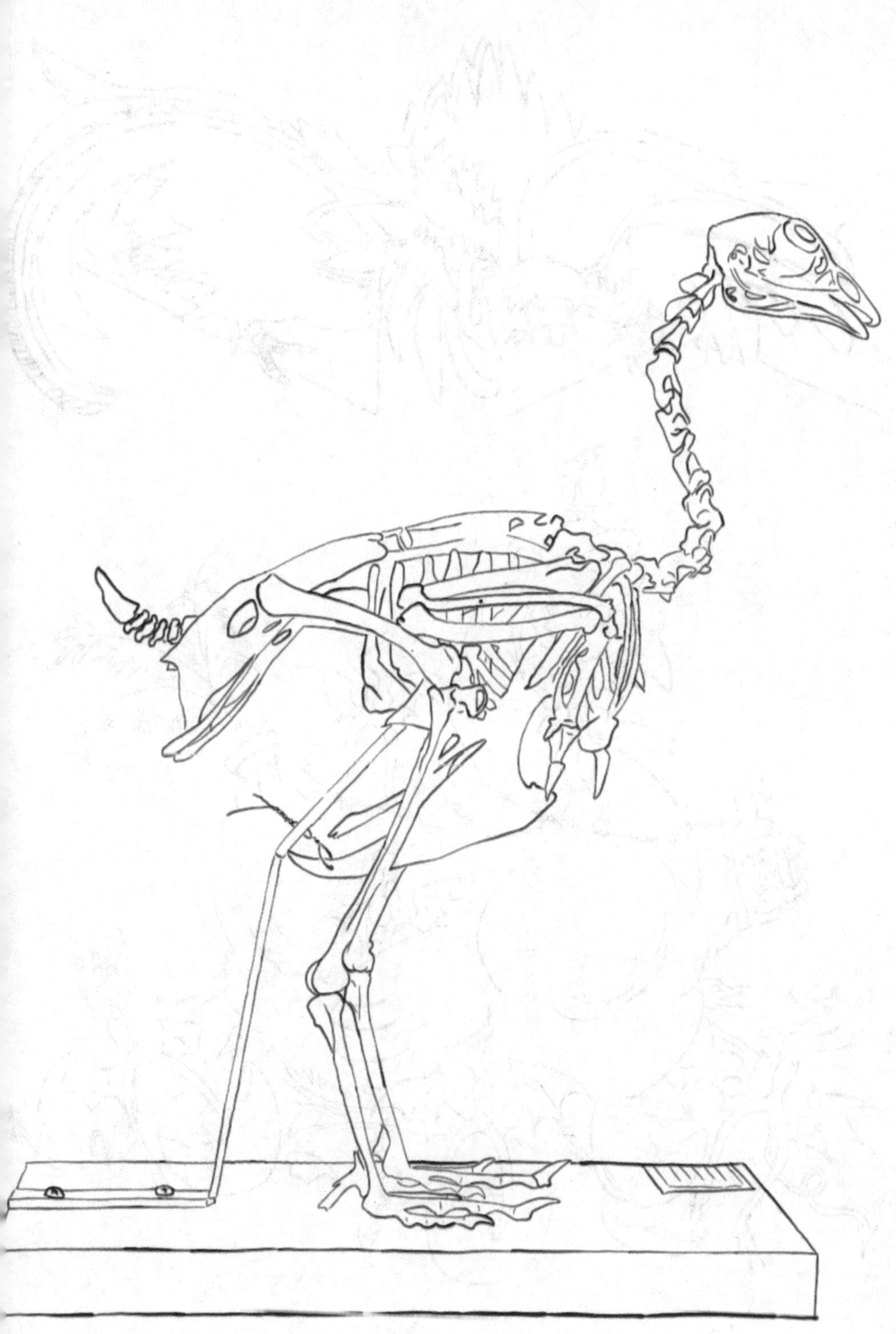

National Museum of Natural History
Title: Red Junglefowl, Chicken
Scientific Name: Gallus gallus
Materials: Complete Skeleton

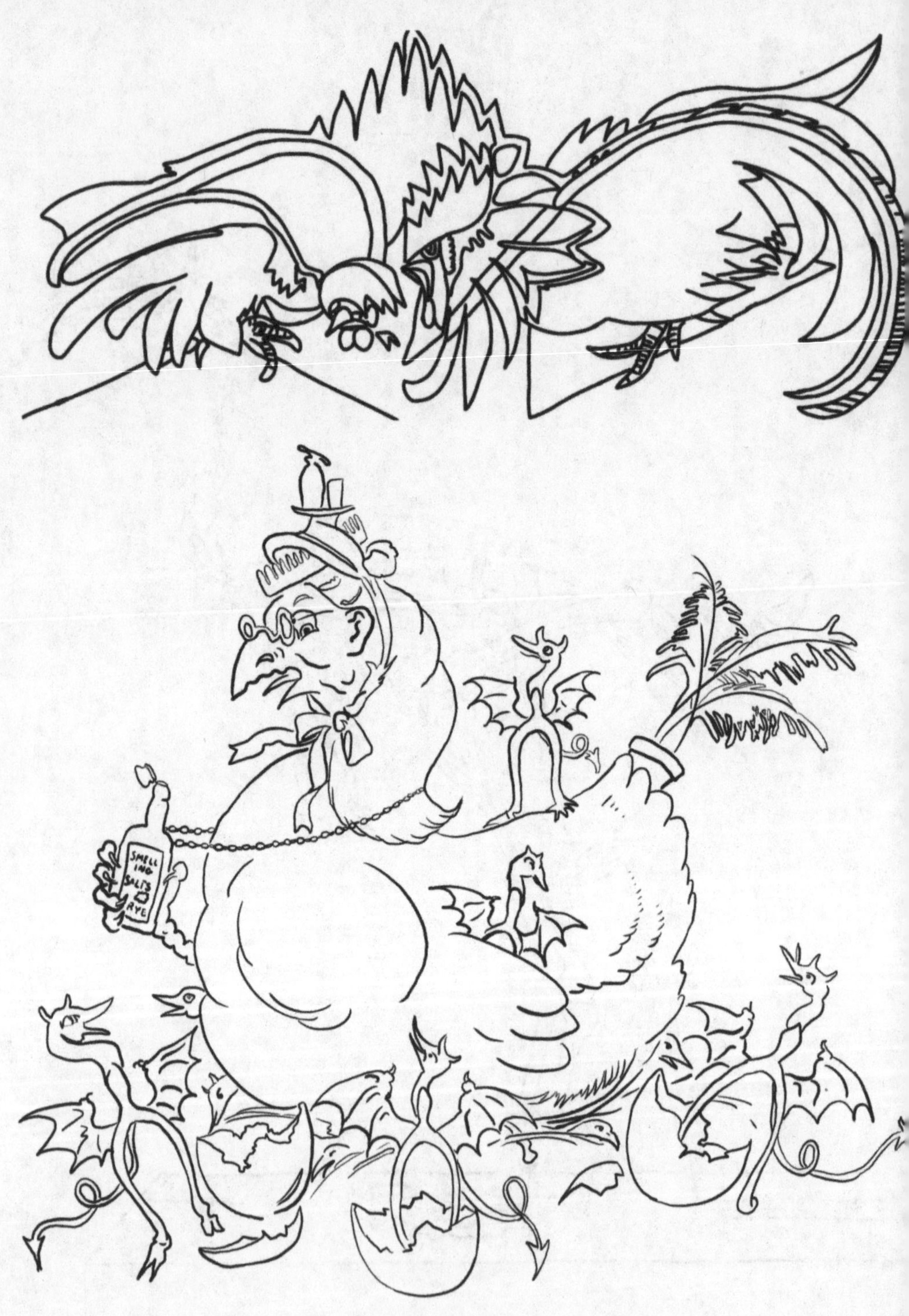

The Art Institute of Chicago
Title: Roosters
Artist: Sekino Jun'ichiro
Meduim: Color woodblock print
Depicted topmost

New York Public Library Digital Collections
Title: Dinner to Old Mother "Wishbone" by Her Spring Chicks [held by]
Cedar Park Dining Club [at] "Philadelphia, PA" (Other (Private Club);)
Artist: Frank Buttoph (Collector)
Medium: Paper and ink
Depicted bottommost

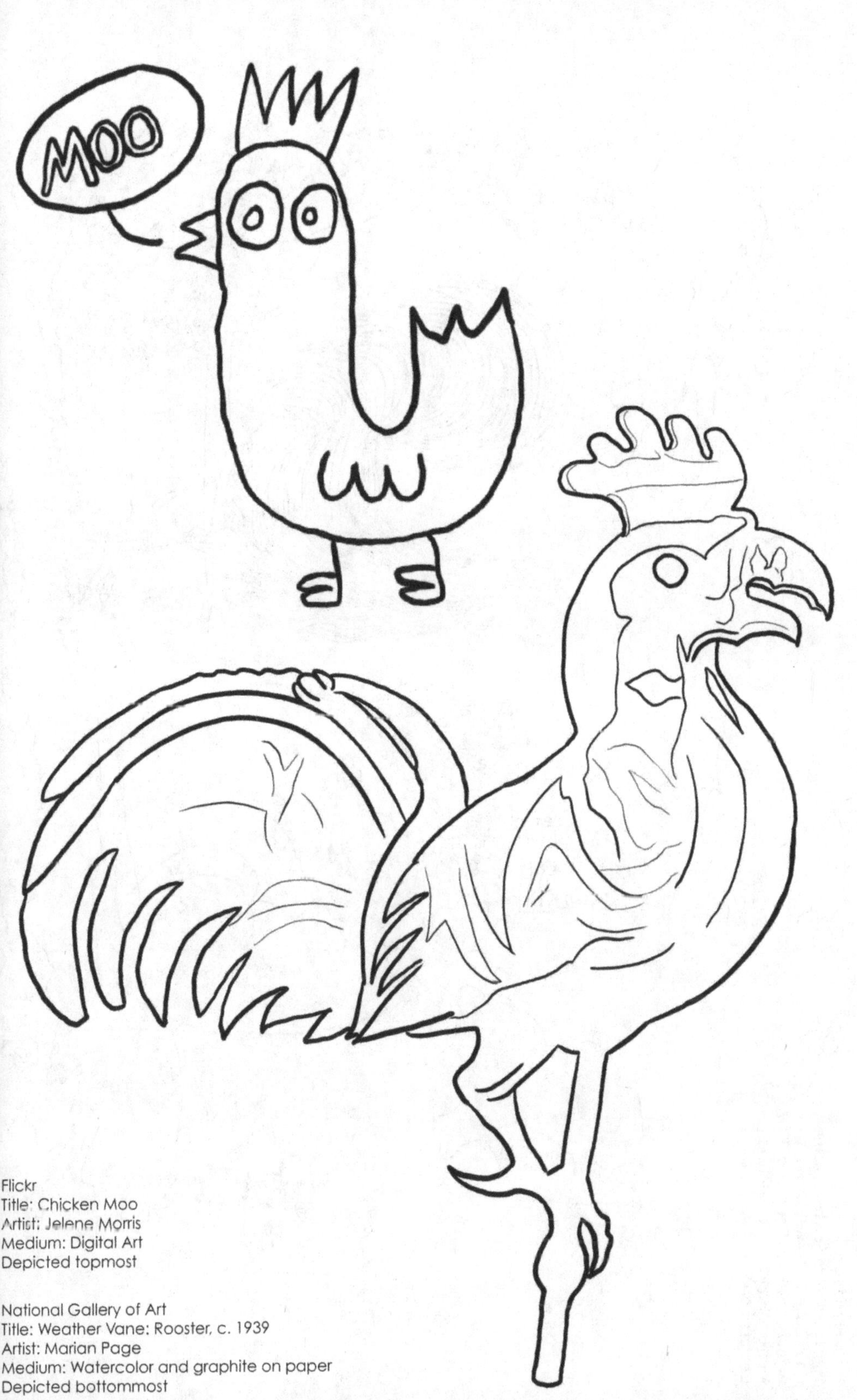

Flickr
Title: Chicken Moo
Artist: Jelene Morris
Medium: Digital Art
Depicted topmost

National Gallery of Art
Title: Weather Vane: Rooster, c. 1939
Artist: Marian Page
Medium: Watercolor and graphite on paper
Depicted bottommost

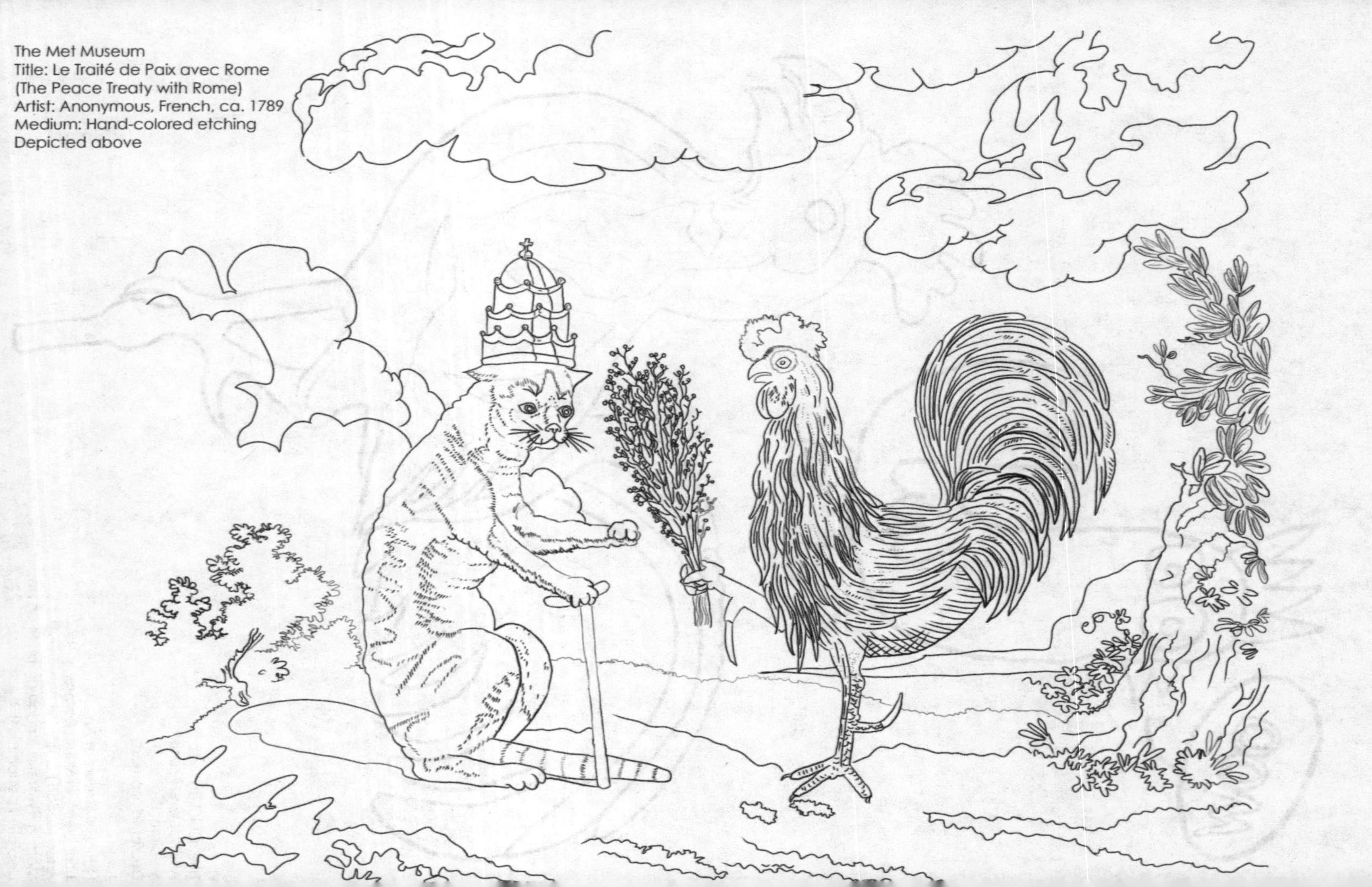

The Met Museum
Title: Le Traité de Paix avec Rome
(The Peace Treaty with Rome)
Artist: Anonymous, French, ca. 1789
Medium: Hand-colored etching
Depicted above

The Met Museum
Title: Boy with an Egg, Girl with a Hen, and a Watching Woman
Artist: Giovanni Battista Piazzetta (Italian, Venice 1682–1754 Venice)
Medium: Charcoal and chalk, on blue-gray paper faded to brown
Depicted below

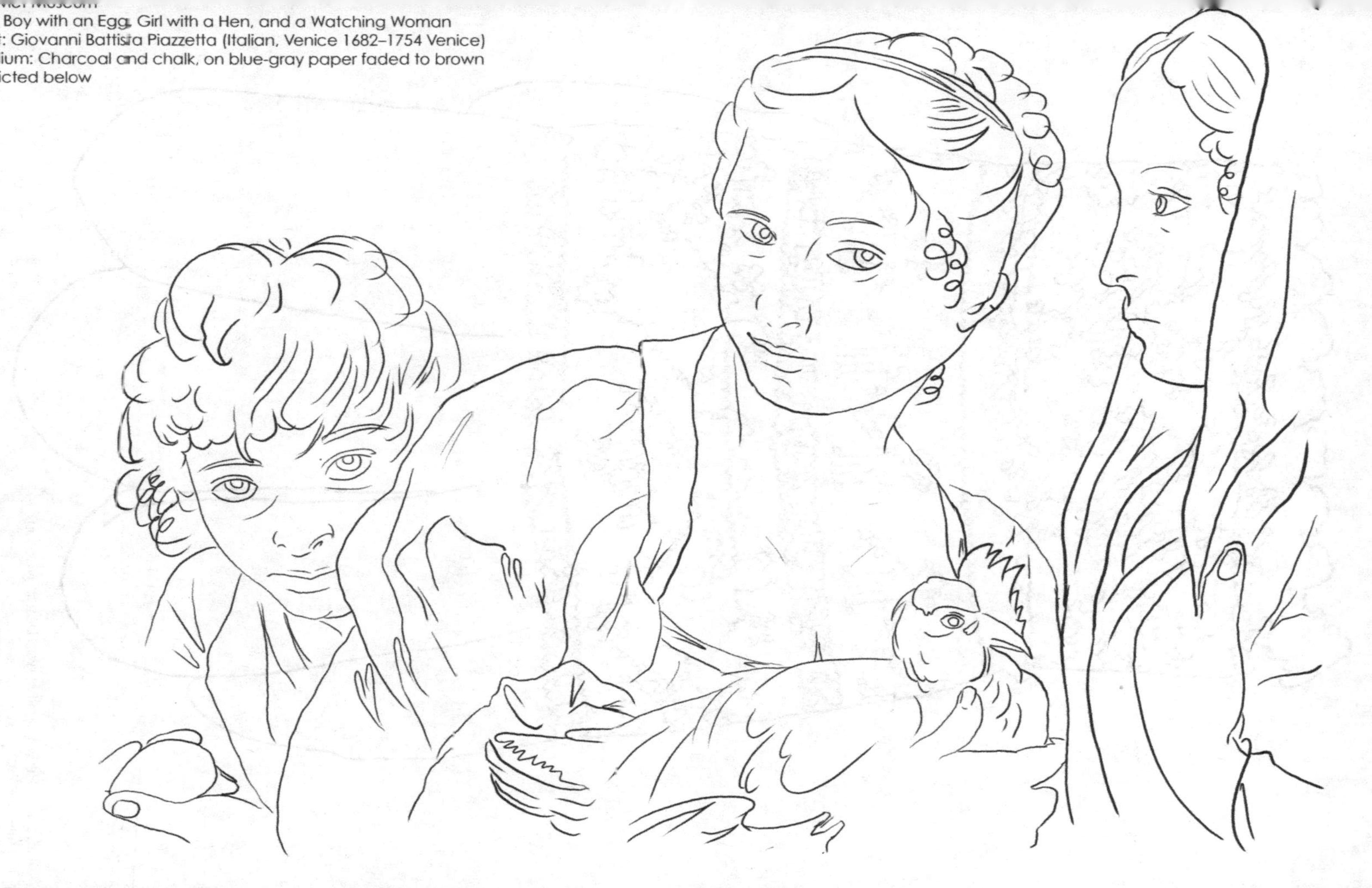

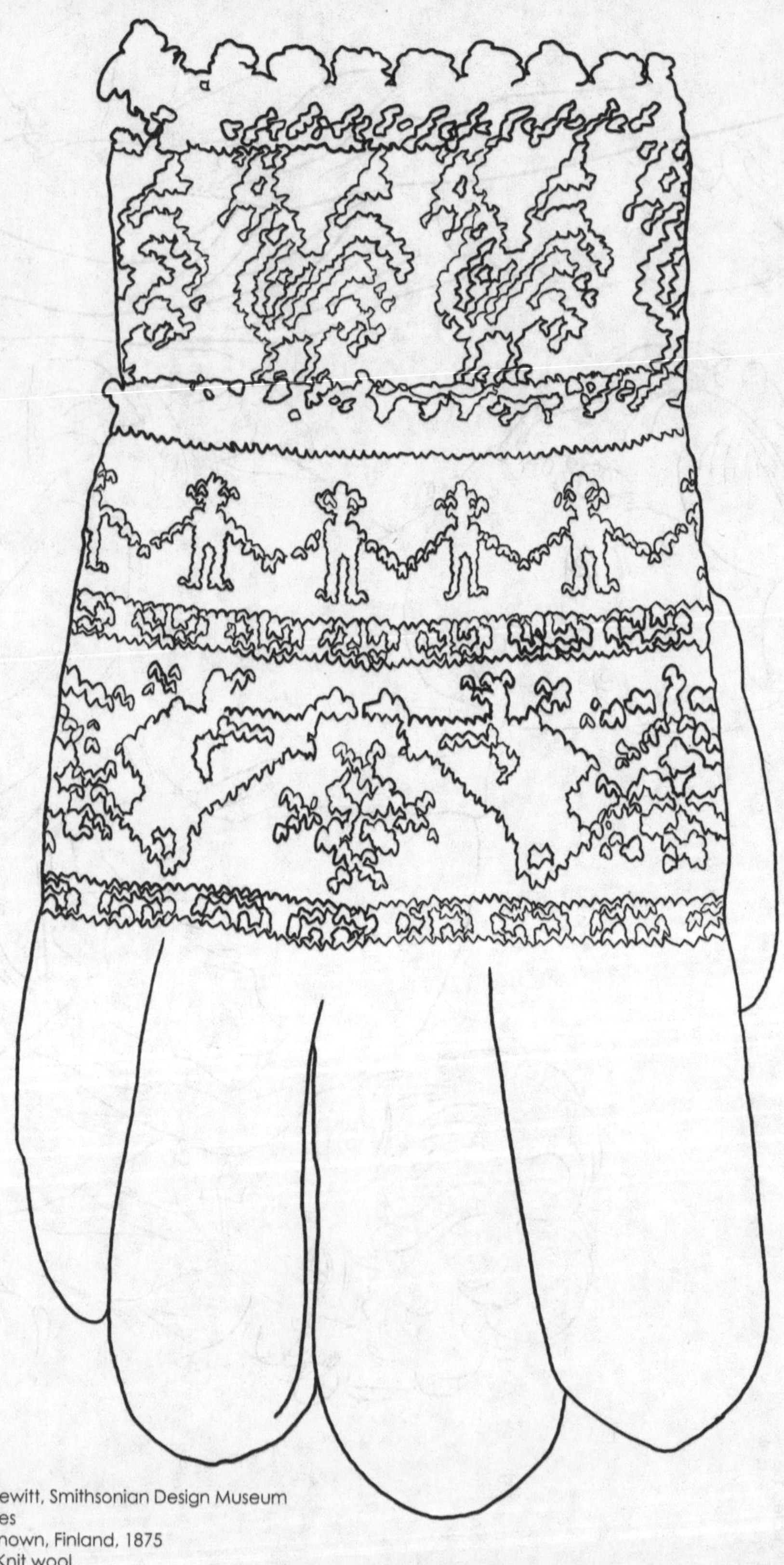

Cooper Hewitt, Smithsonian Design Museum
Title: Gloves
Artist: Unknown, Finland, 1875
Medium: Knit wool

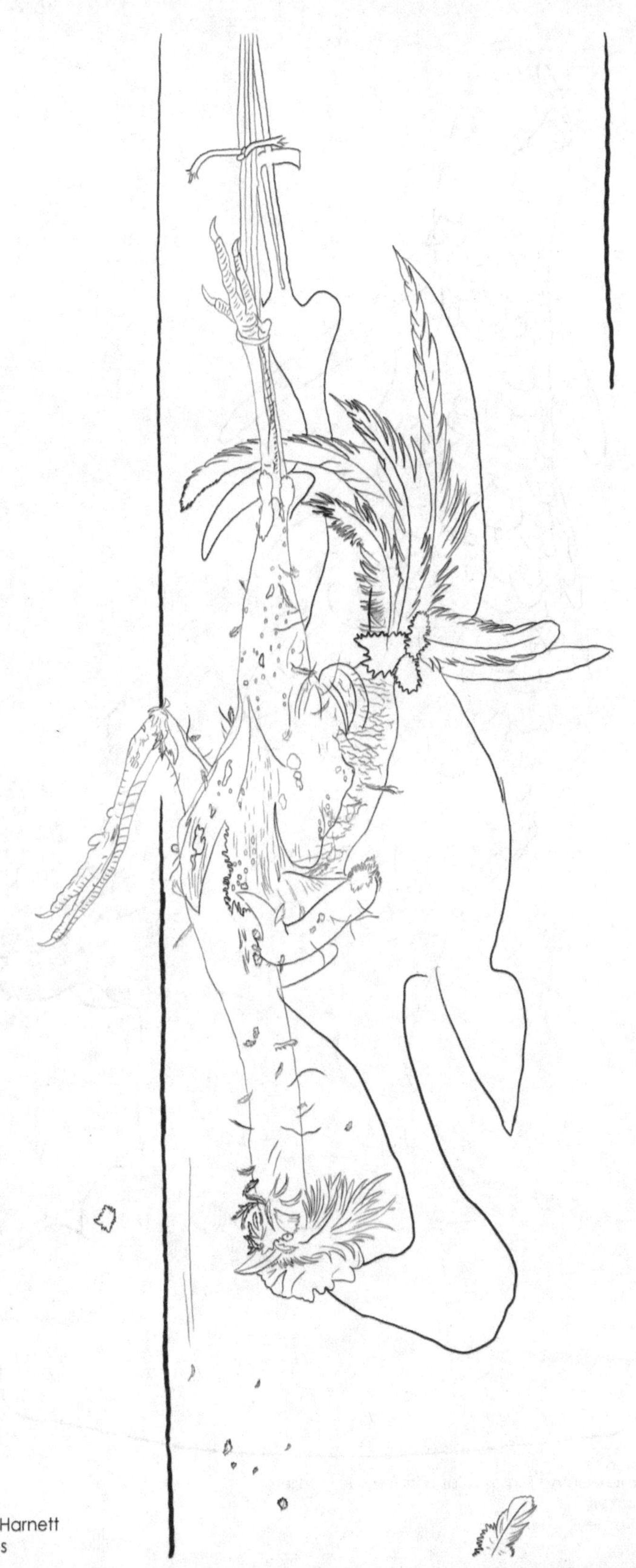

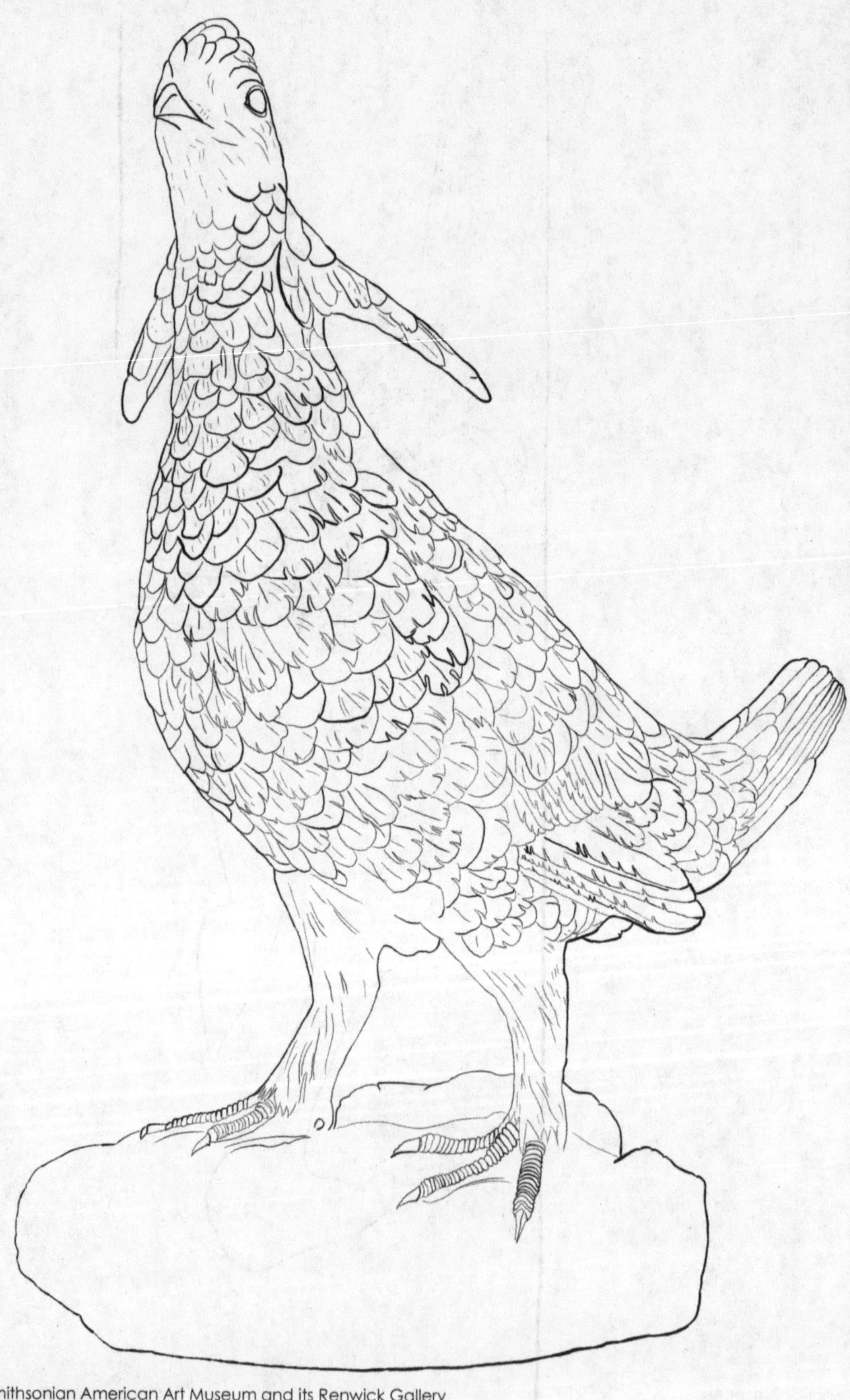

Smithsonian American Art Museum and its Renwick Gallery
Title: Prairie Chicken
Artist: Edward Kemeys
Medium: Metal

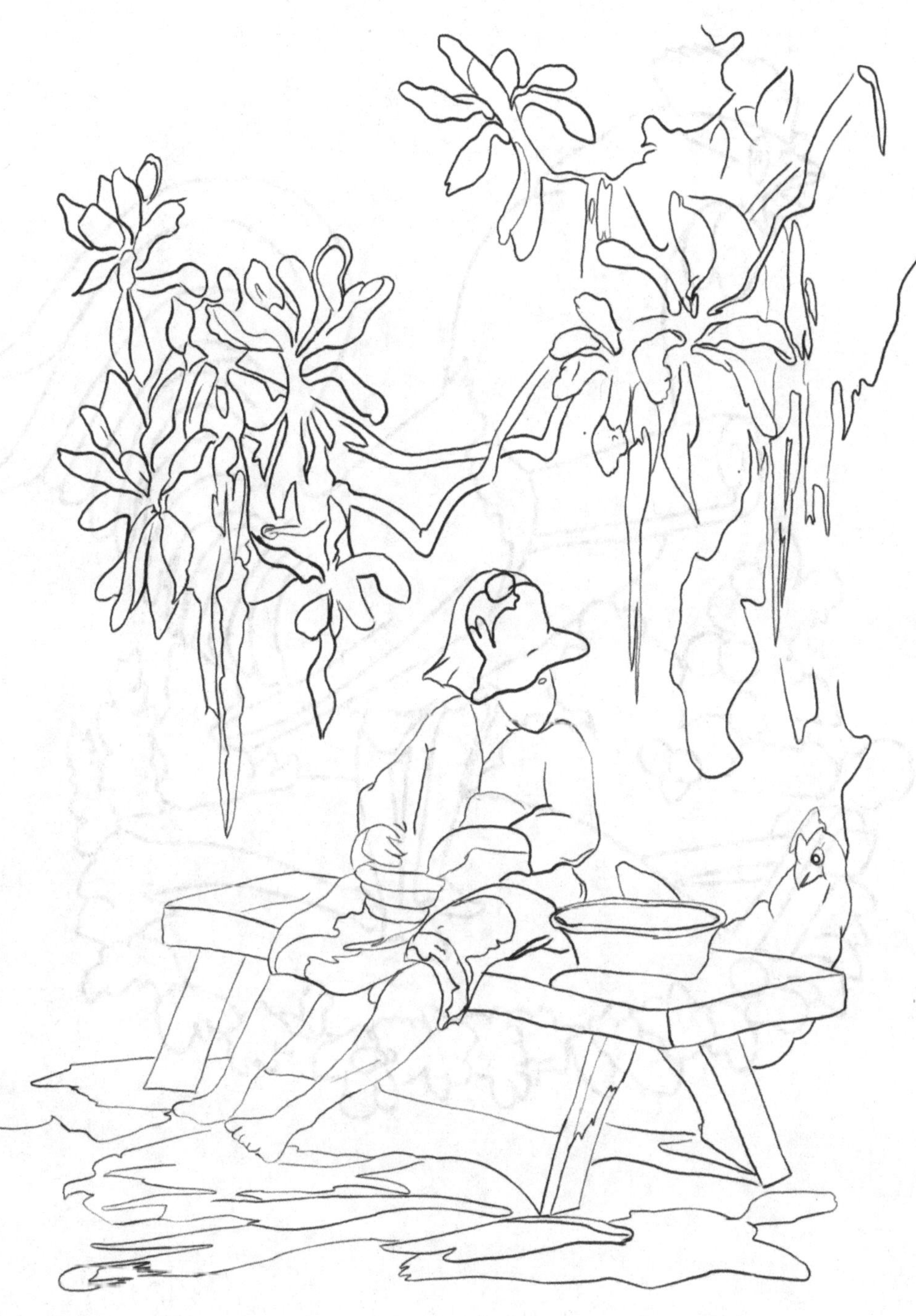

Smithsonian American Art Museum and its Renwick Gallery
Title: Little Miss Muffet
Artist: Helen Hyde, born Lima,
Medium: Color etching and aquatint on paper

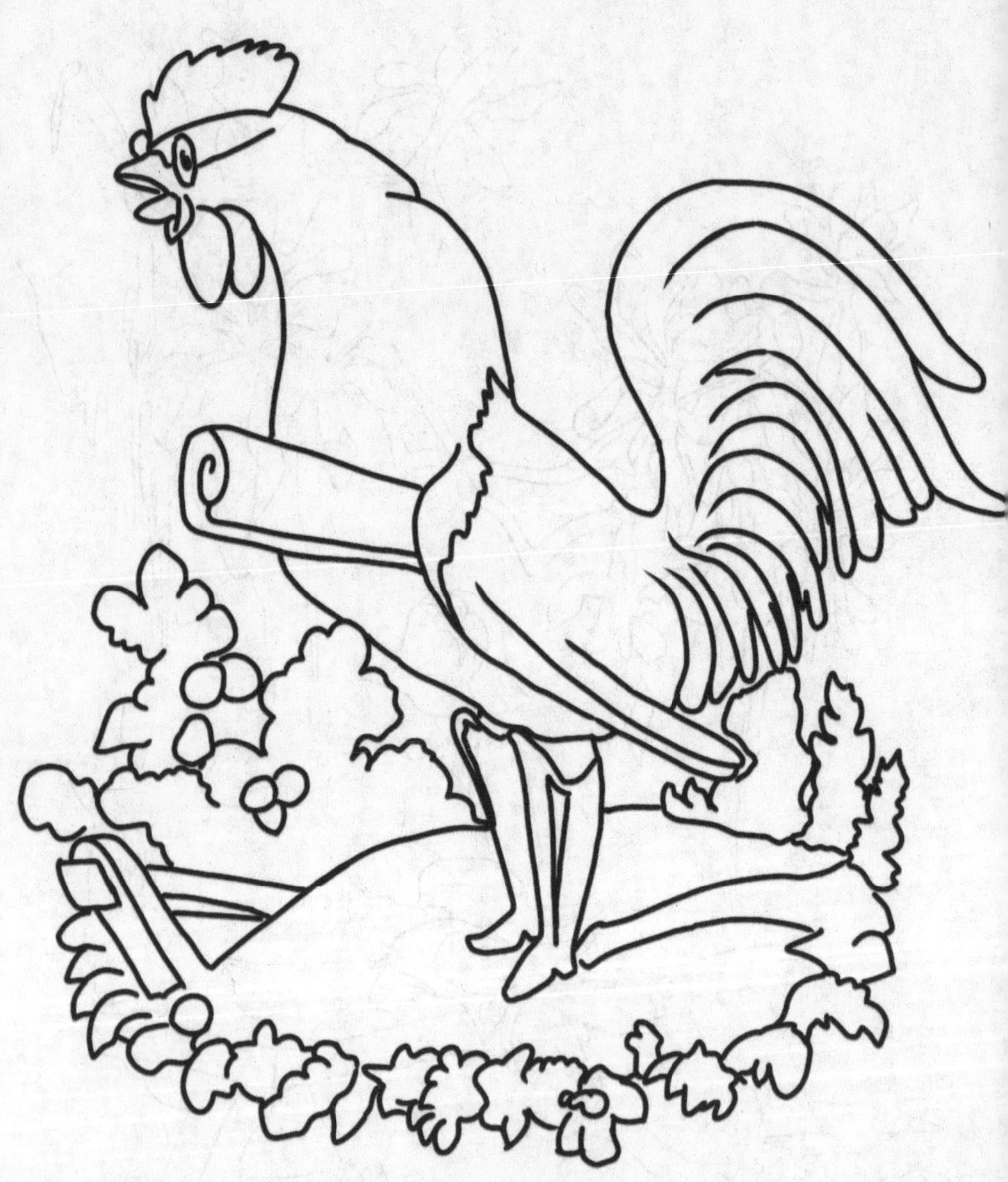

The Met Museum
Title: Valentine
Artist: Anonymous, ca.1850–70
Medium: Cameo-embossed lace paper, chromolithography

A TOUGH CHICK.

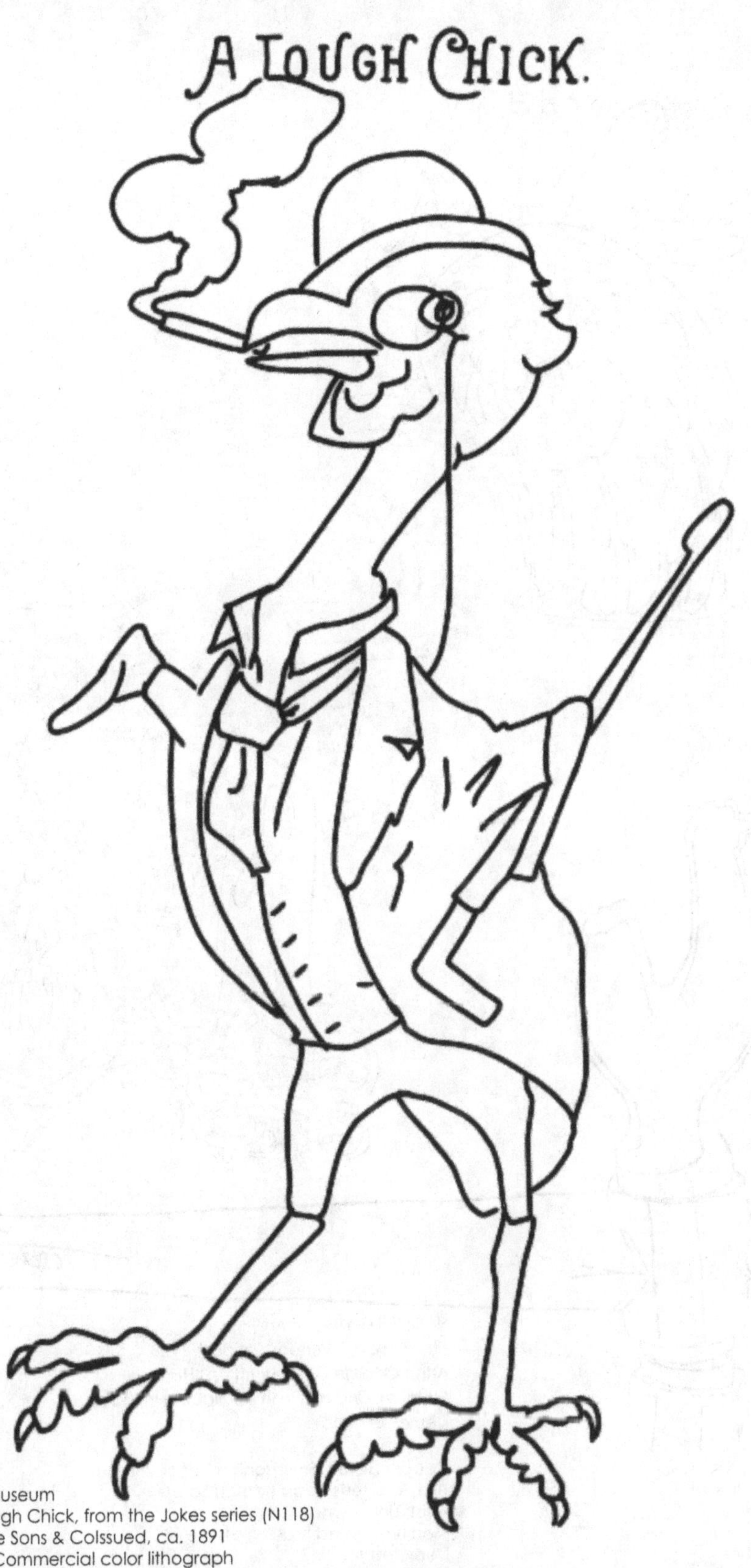

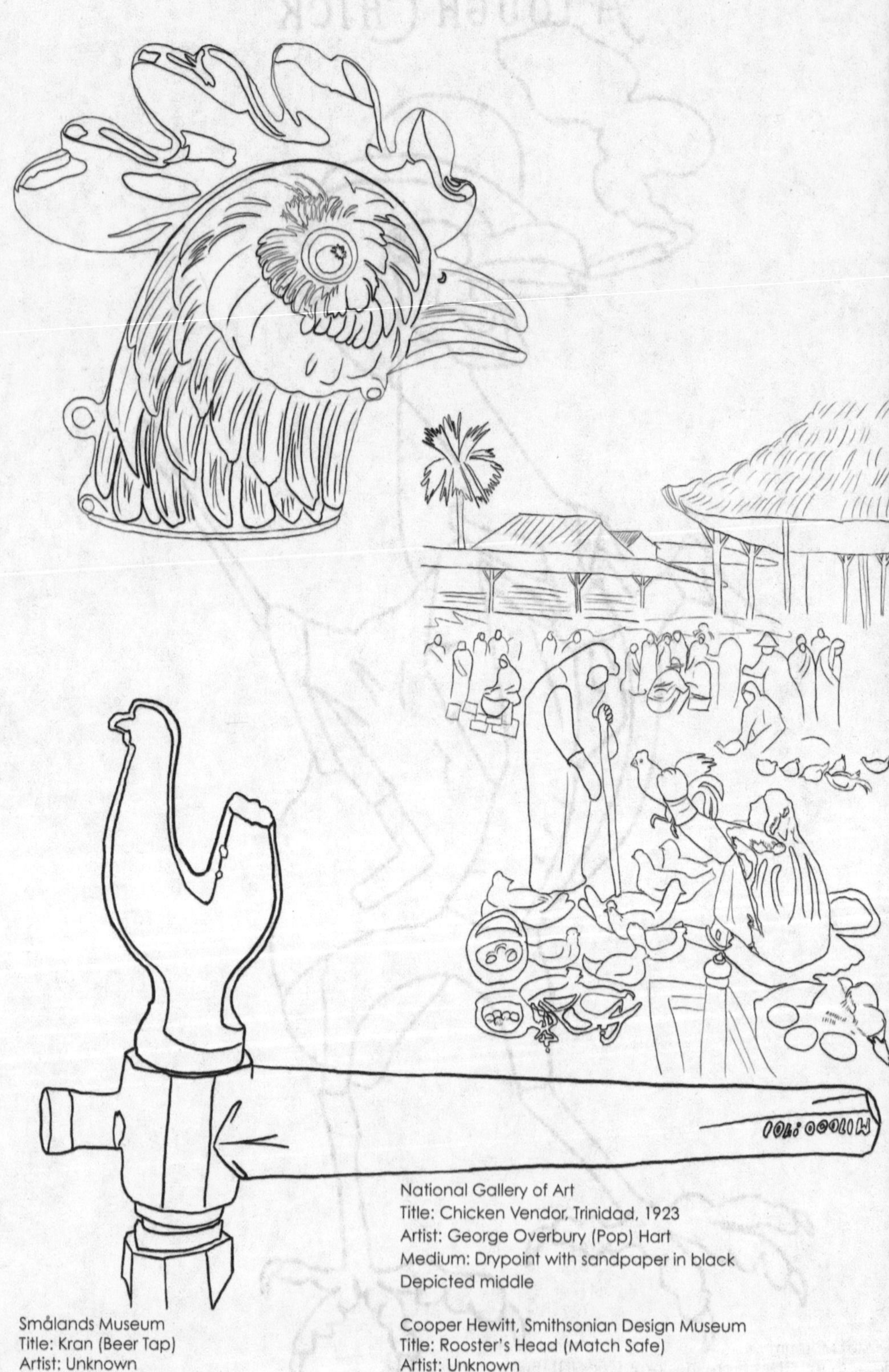

National Gallery of Art
Title: Chicken Vendor, Trinidad, 1923
Artist: George Overbury (Pop) Hart
Medium: Drypoint with sandpaper in black
Depicted middle

Smålands Museum
Title: Kran (Beer Tap)
Artist: Unknown
Medium: Bronze
Depicted bottom

Cooper Hewitt, Smithsonian Design Museum
Title: Rooster's Head (Match Safe)
Artist: Unknown
Medium: Plated brass, glass
Depicted top

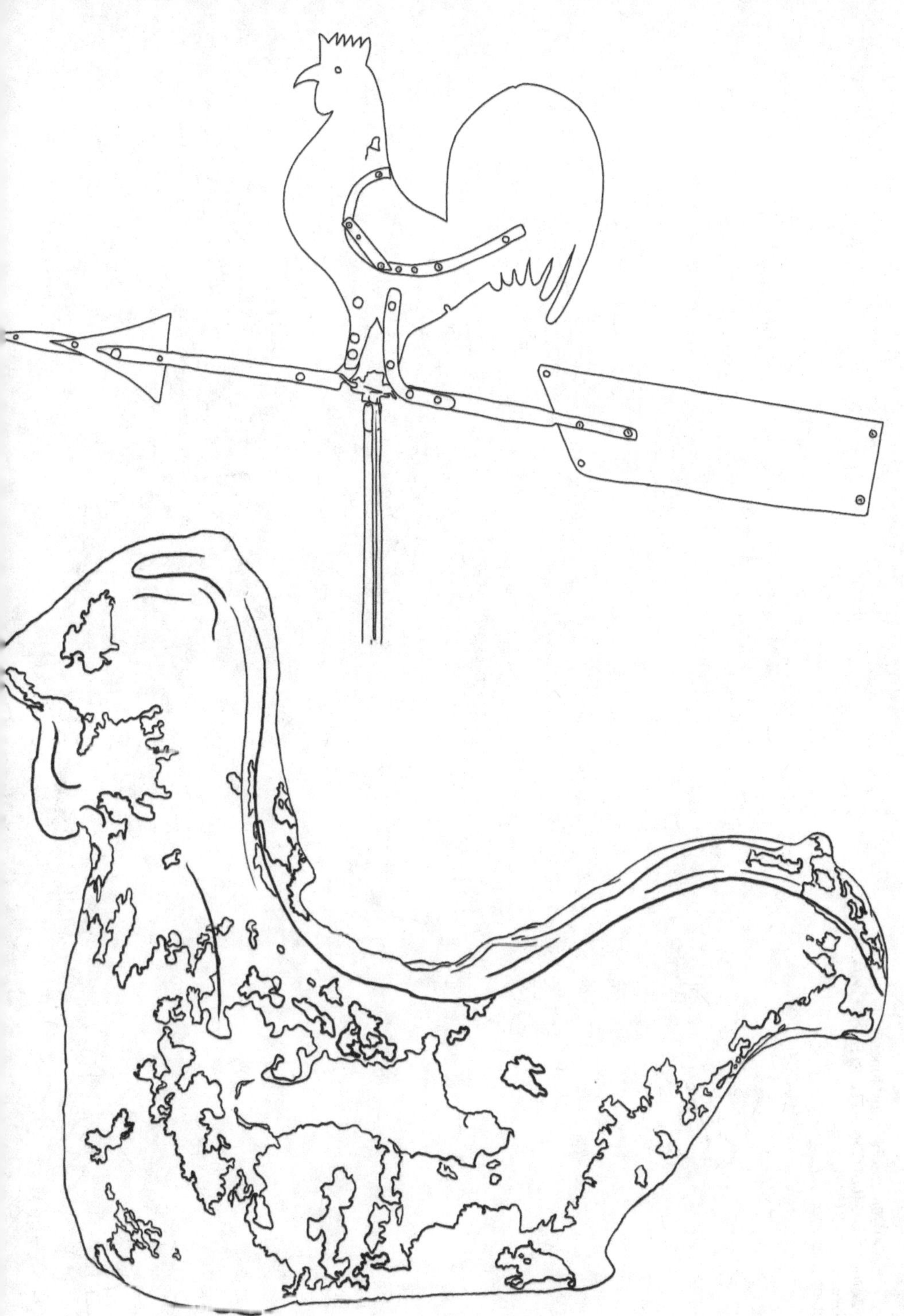

Smithsonian American Art Museum and its
Renwick Gallery
Title: Rooster Weathervane
Artist: Unknown, American 19th Century
Medium: Sheet and wrought iron
Depicted topmost

National Museum of Asian Art, Smithsonian Institution
Title: Tomb figure of a chicken, Freer Collection, Gift of
Charles Lang Freer, F1906.245
Artist: Unknown, China, early 1st-early 3rd century
Medium: Earthenware with copper-green lead-silicate glaze
Depicted bottommost

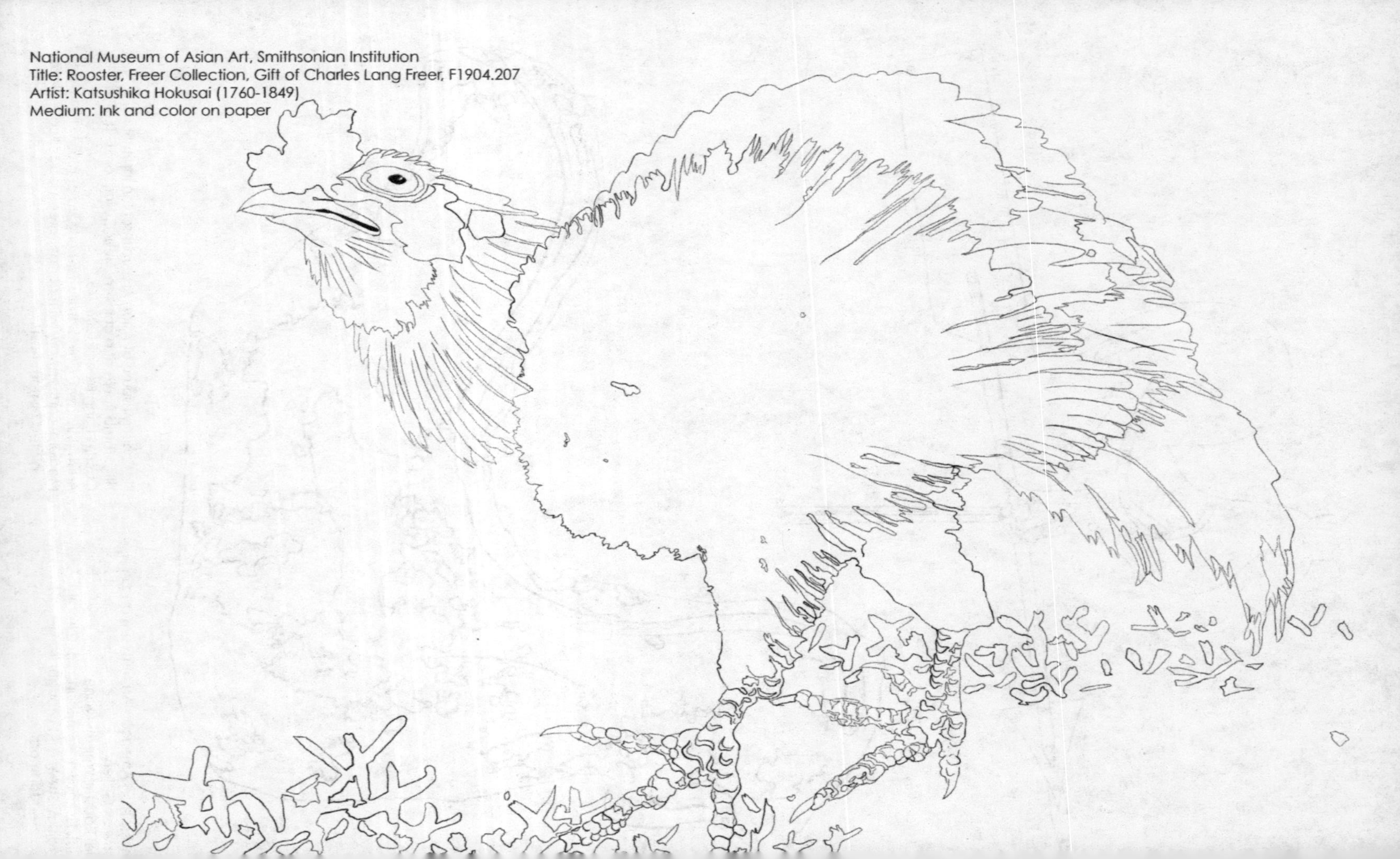

National Museum of Asian Art, Smithsonian Institution
Title: Rooster, Freer Collection, Gift of Charles Lang Freer, F1904.207
Artist: Katsushika Hokusai (1760-1849)
Medium: Ink and color on paper

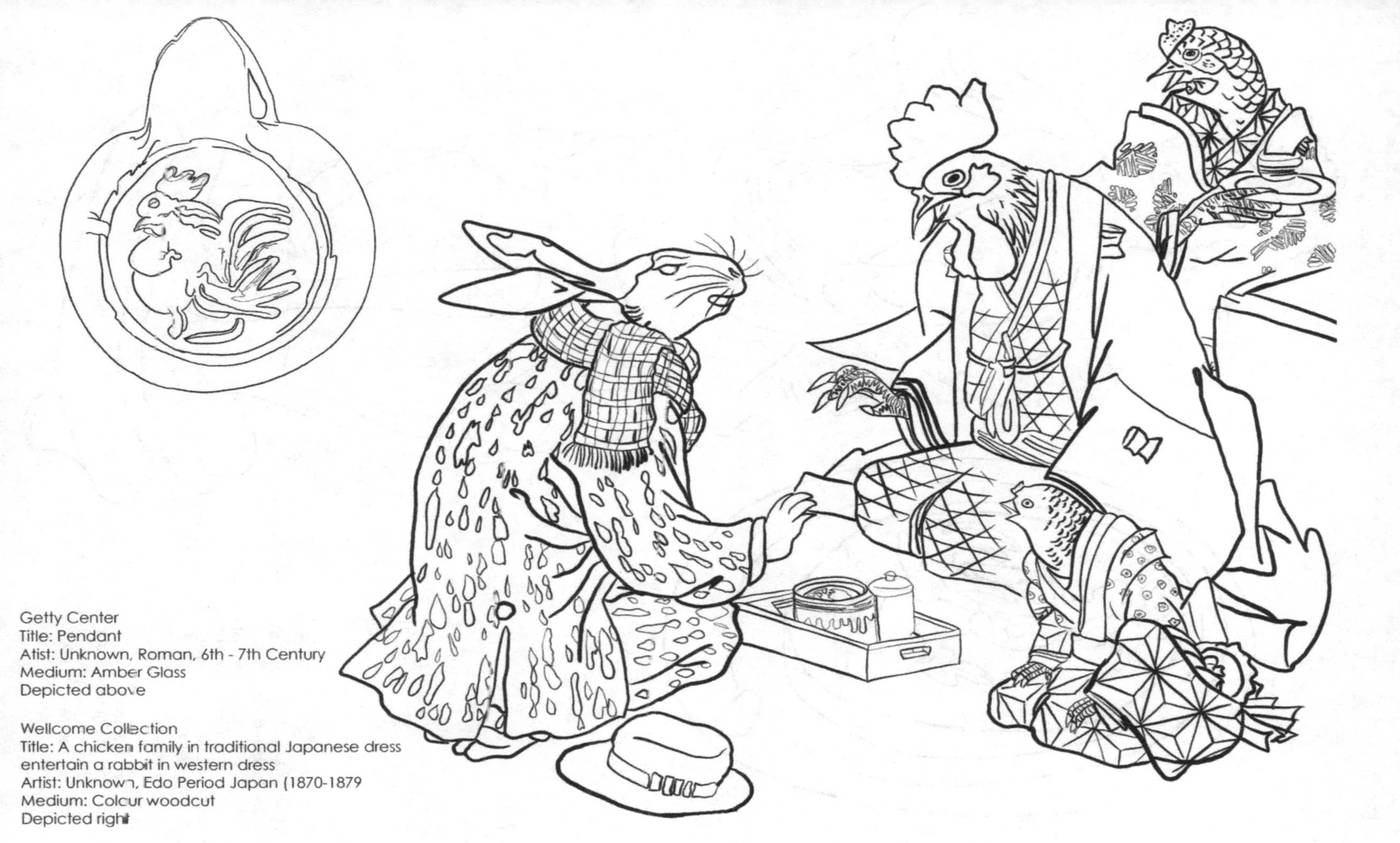

Getty Center
Title: Pendant
Atist: Unknown, Roman, 6th - 7th Century
Medium: Amber Glass
Depicted above

Wellcome Collection
Title: A chicken family in traditional Japanese dress
entertain a rabbit in western dress
Artist: Unknown, Edo Period Japan (1870-1879
Medium: Colcur woodcut
Depicted right

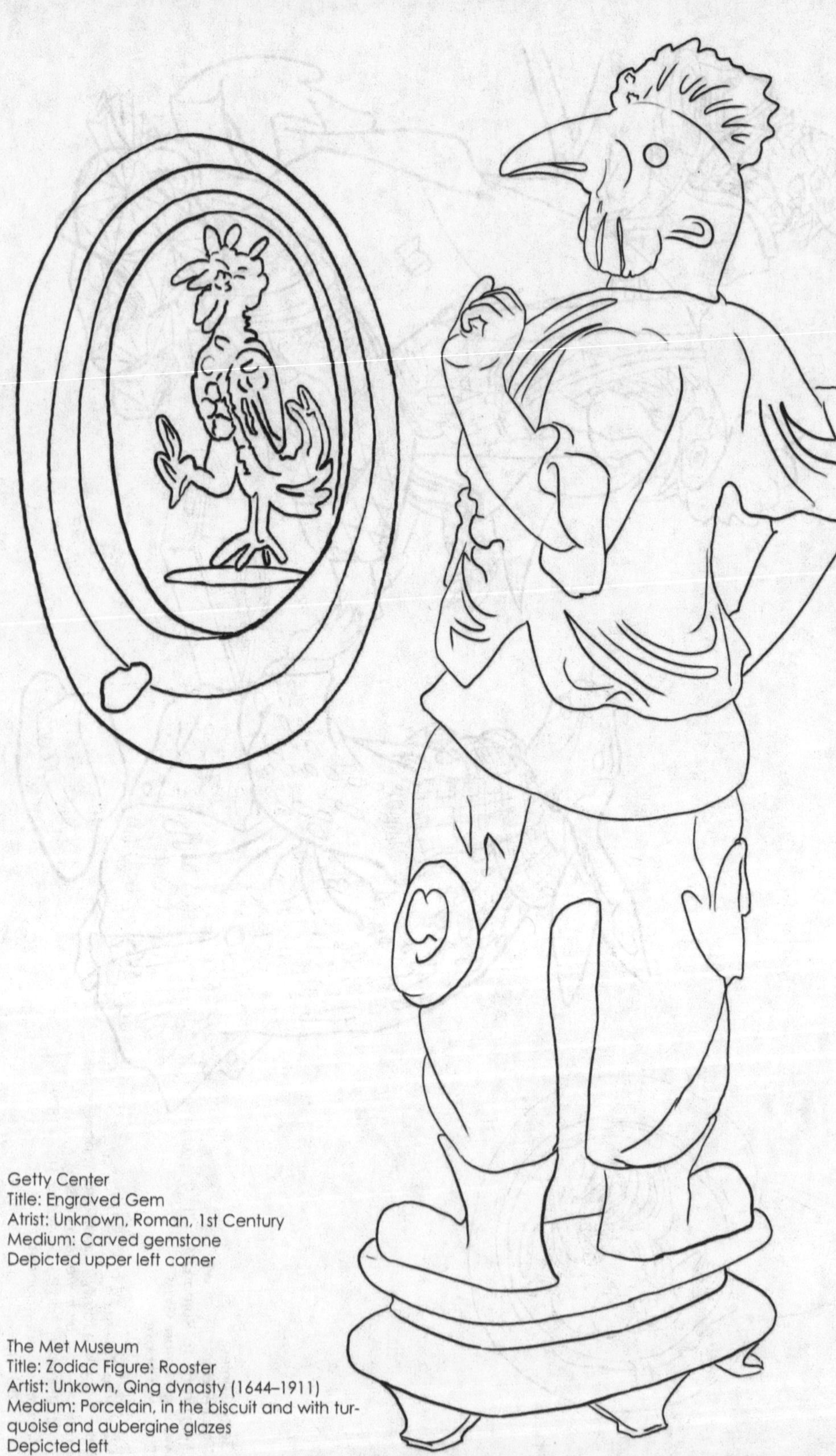

Getty Center
Title: Engraved Gem
Atrist: Unkown, Roman, 1st Century
Medium: Carved gemstone
Depicted upper left corner

The Met Museum
Title: Zodiac Figure: Rooster
Artist: Unkown, Qing dynasty (1644–1911)
Medium: Porcelain, in the biscuit and with tur-
quoise and aubergine glazes
Depicted left

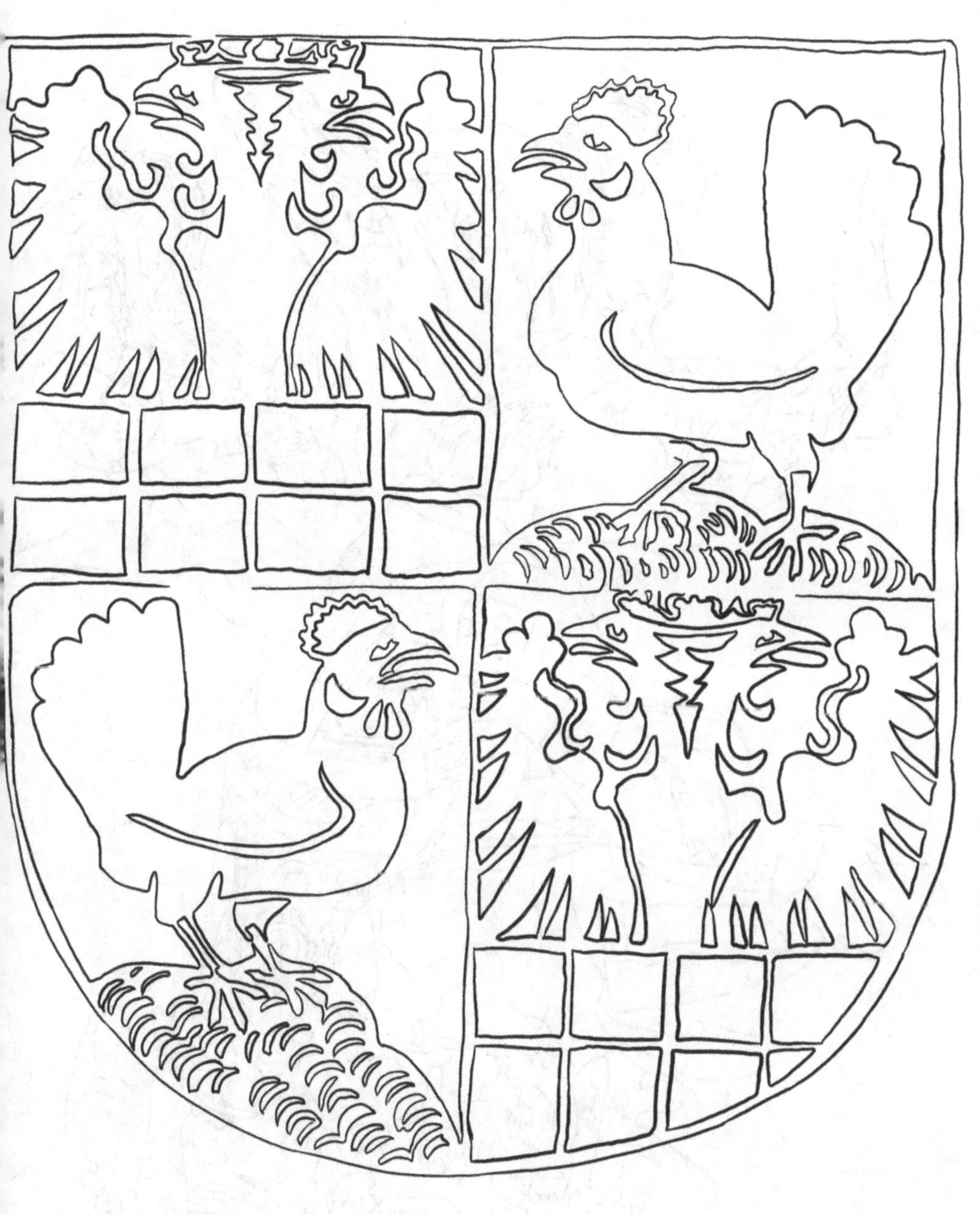

The Met Museum
Title: Arms of the Counts of Botenlauben
Artist: Anonymous, German, Thuringia, 15th century
Medium: Woodcut, colored by stencil

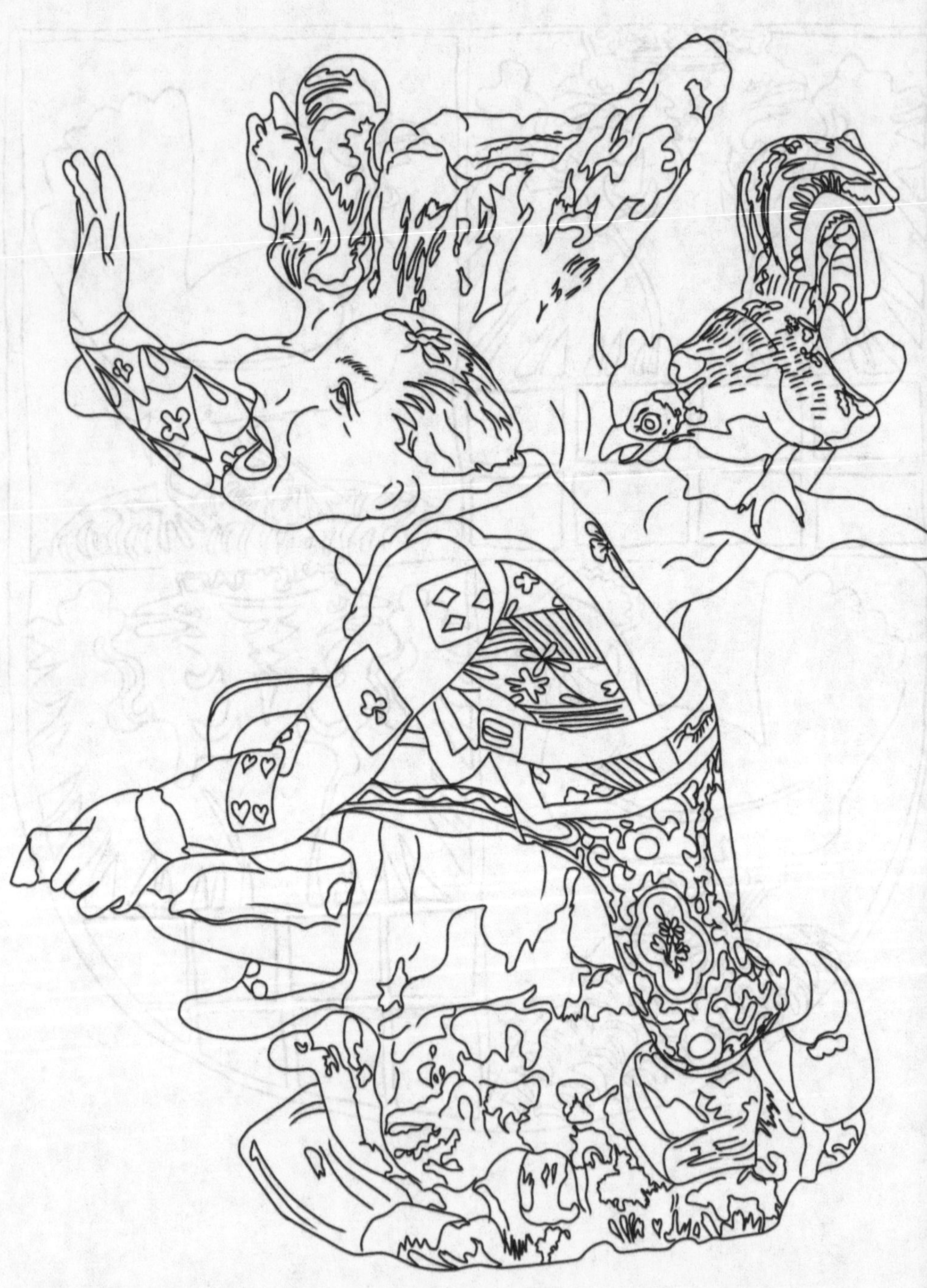

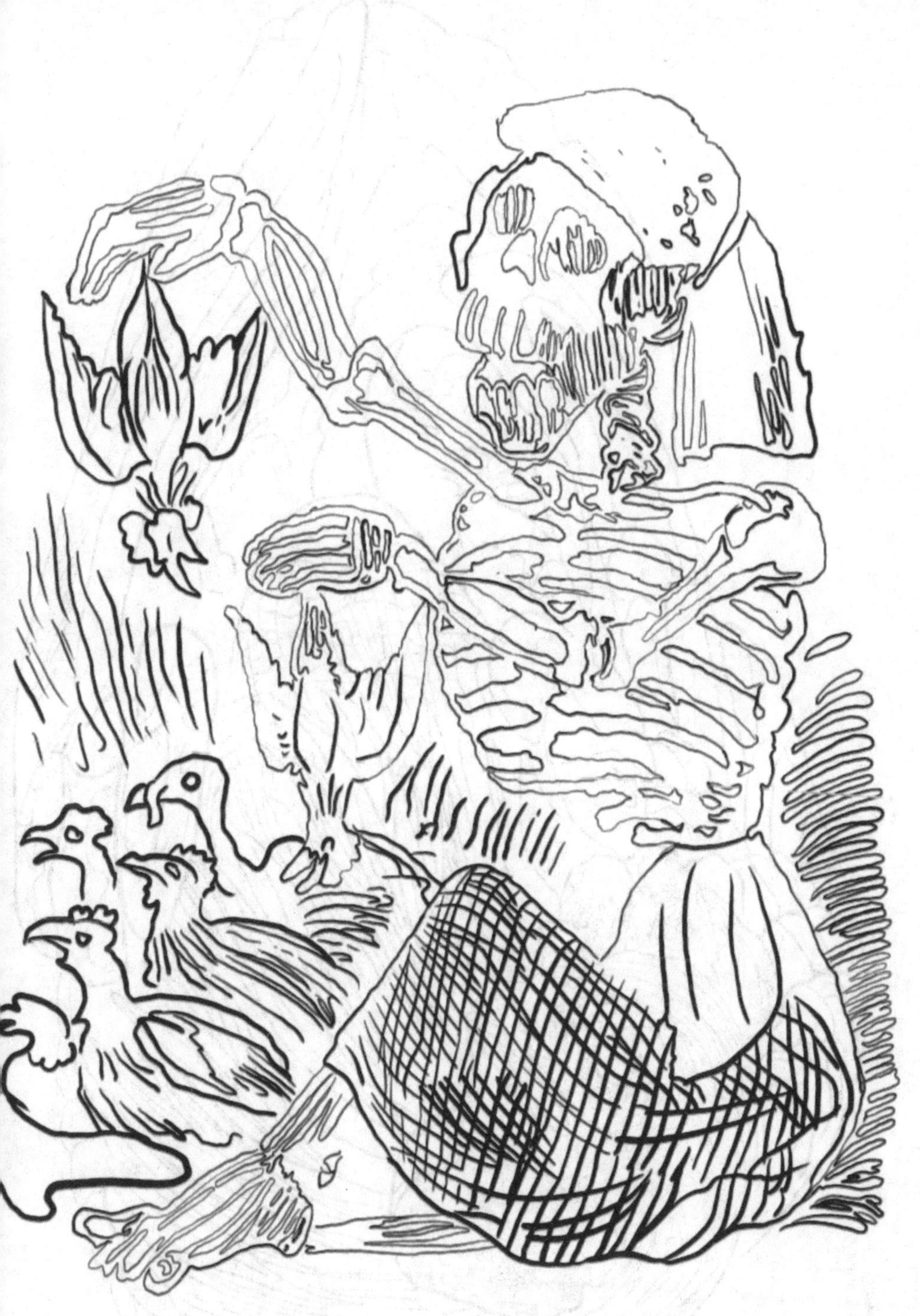

The Met Museum
Title: 'Una Calavera Chusca'
Artist: José Guadalupe Posada
Medium: Zincograph

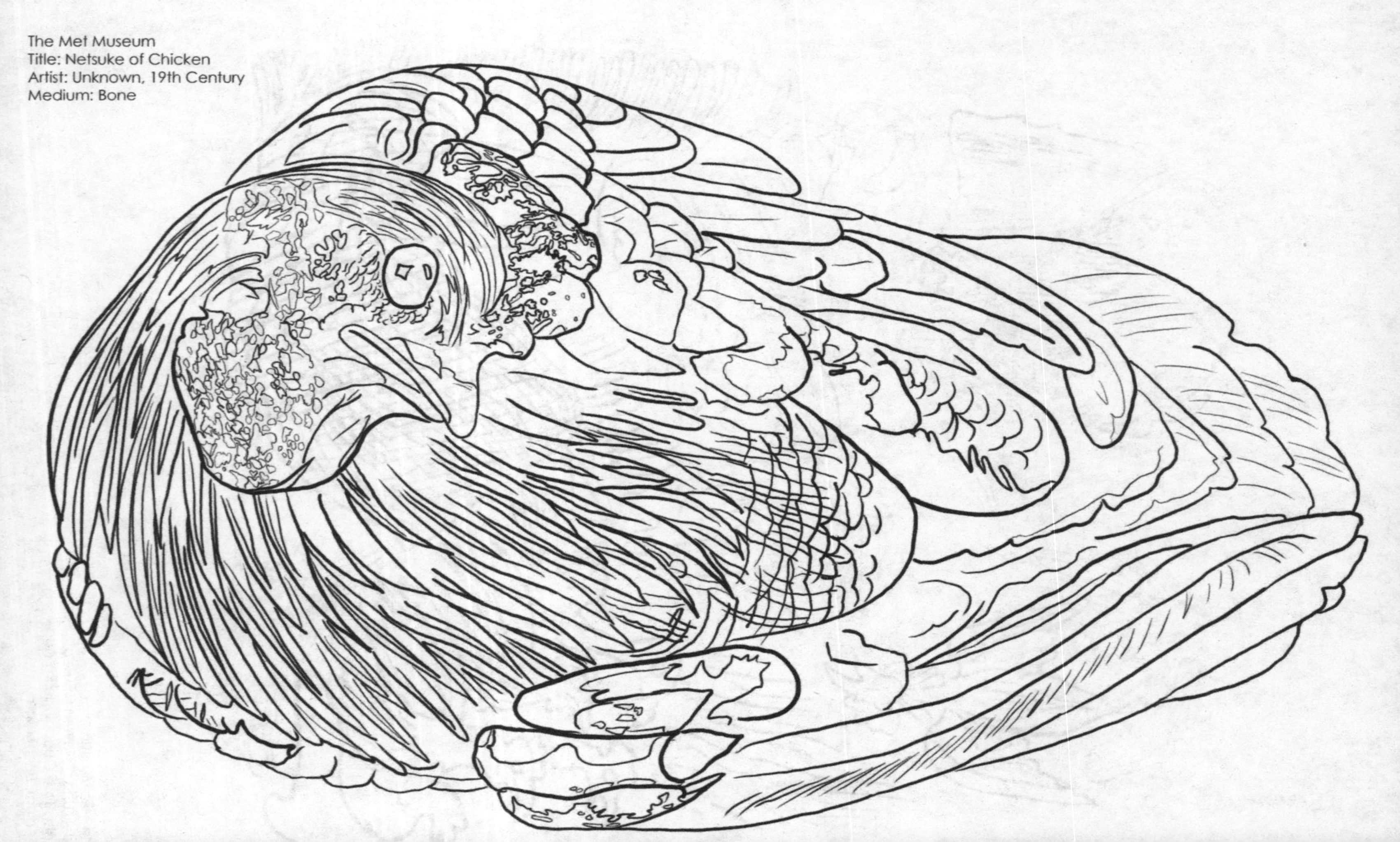

The Met Museum
Title: Netsuke of Chicken
Artist: Unknown, 19th Century
Medium: Bone

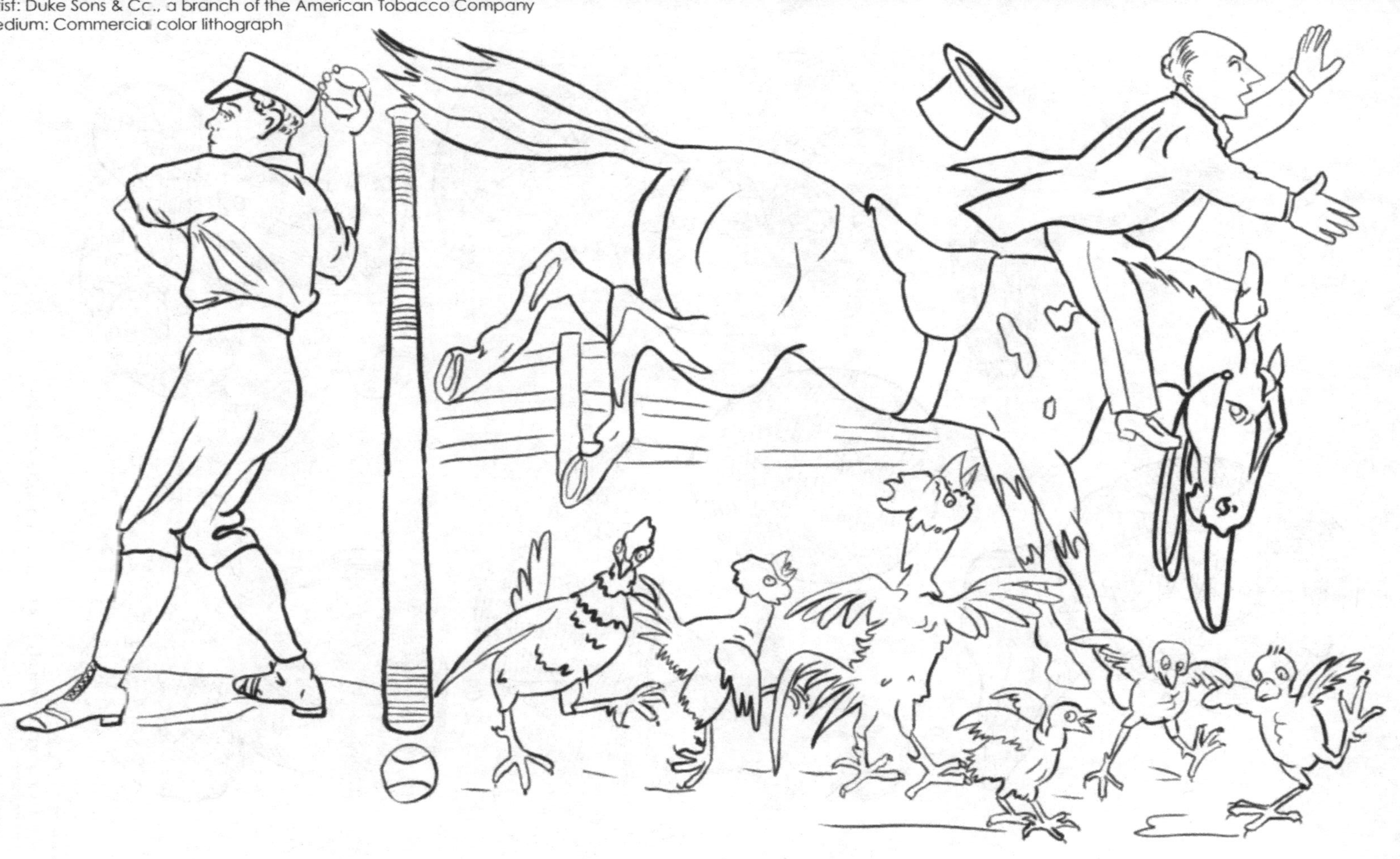

Artist: Duke Sons & Co., a branch of the American Tobacco Company
Medium: Commercial color lithograph

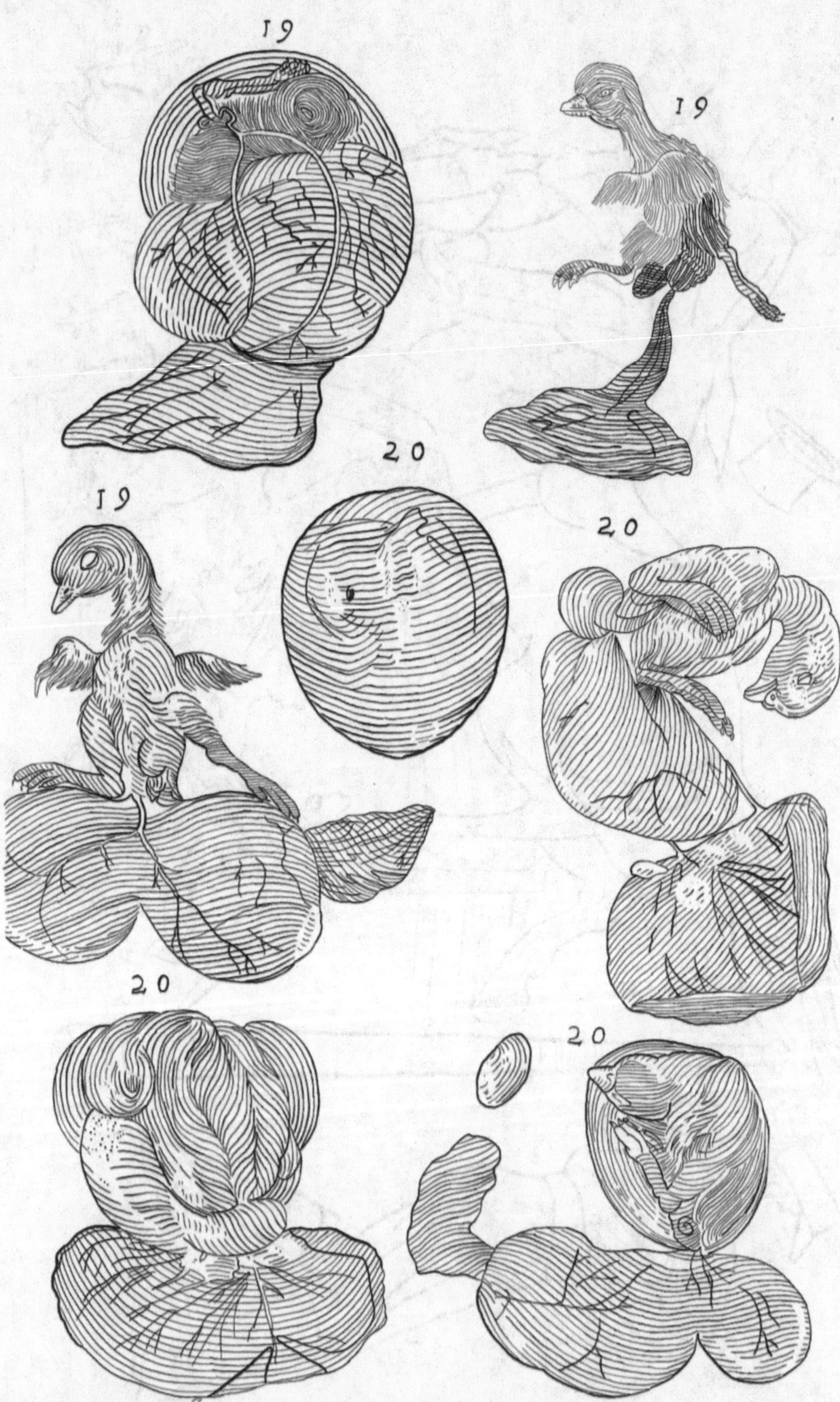

19
19
19
20
20
20
20

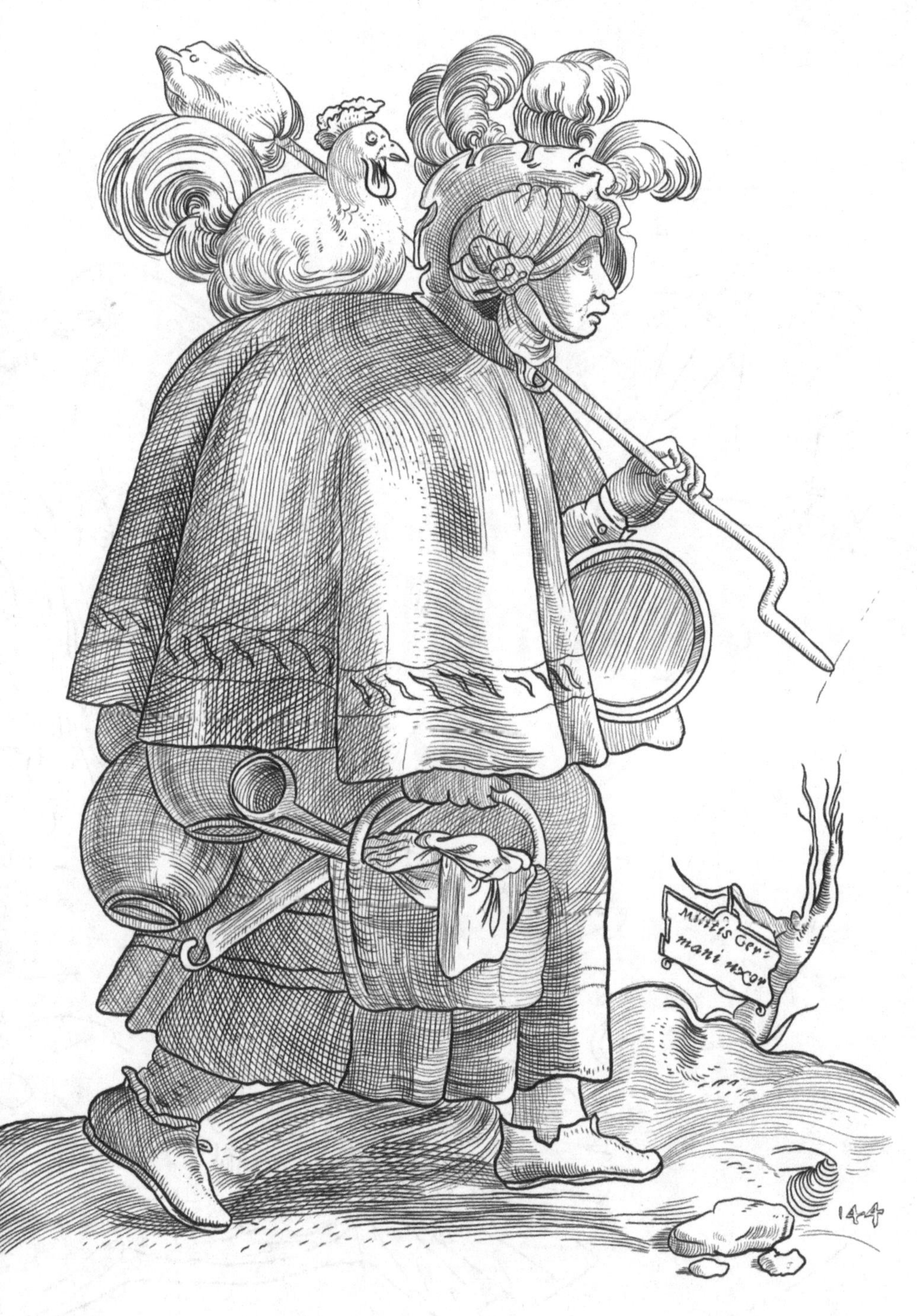
Militis Ger:
mani uxor

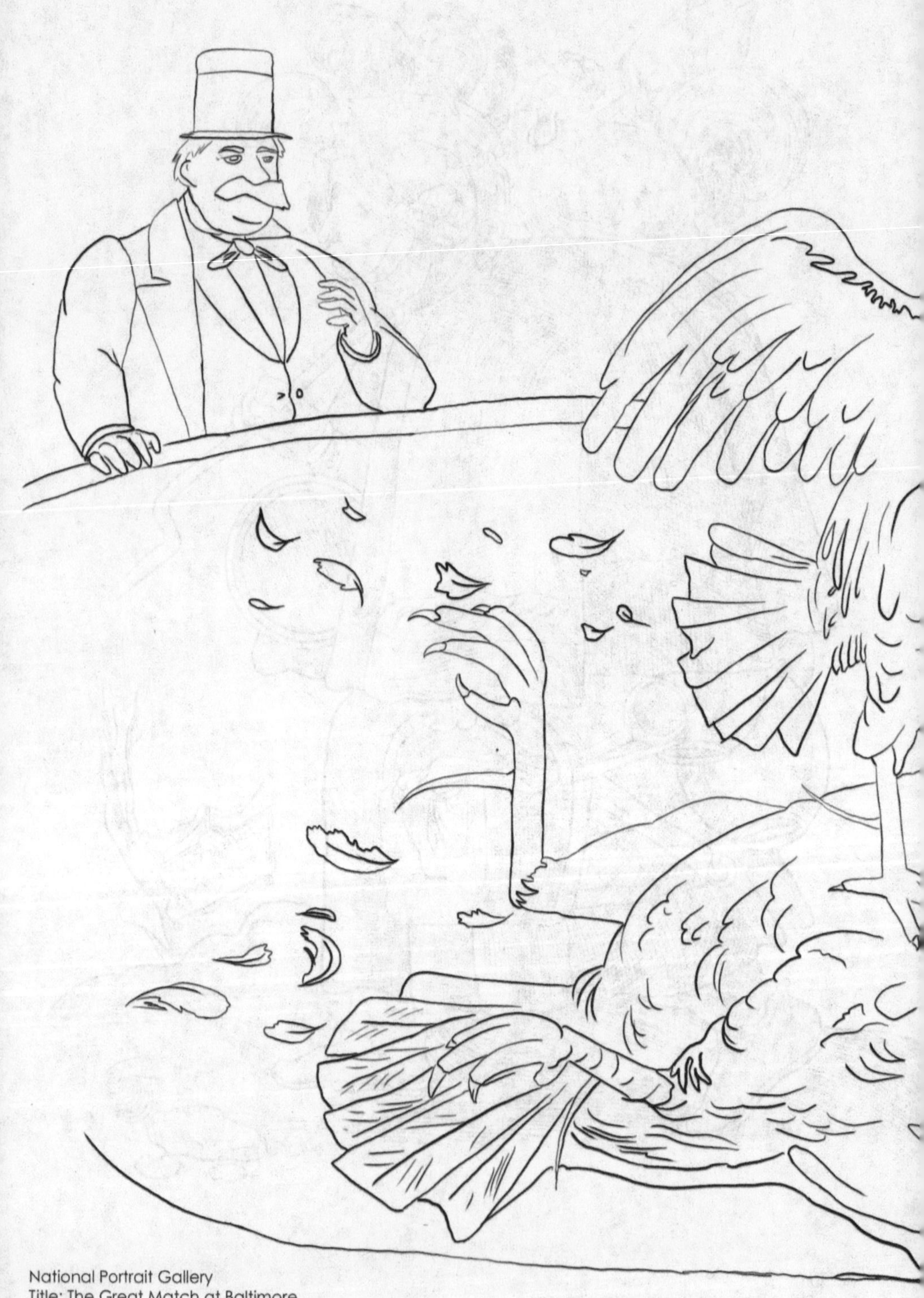

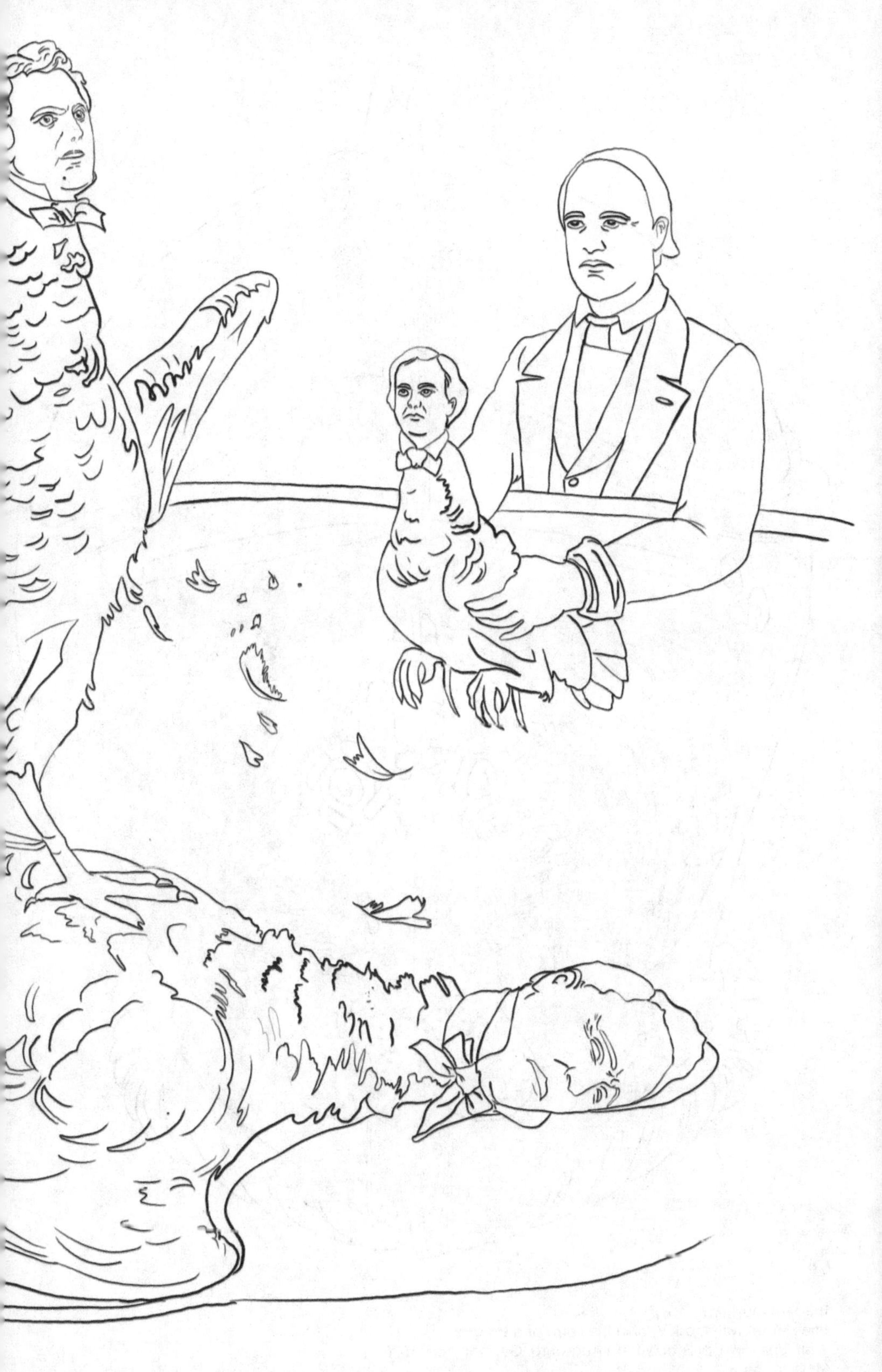

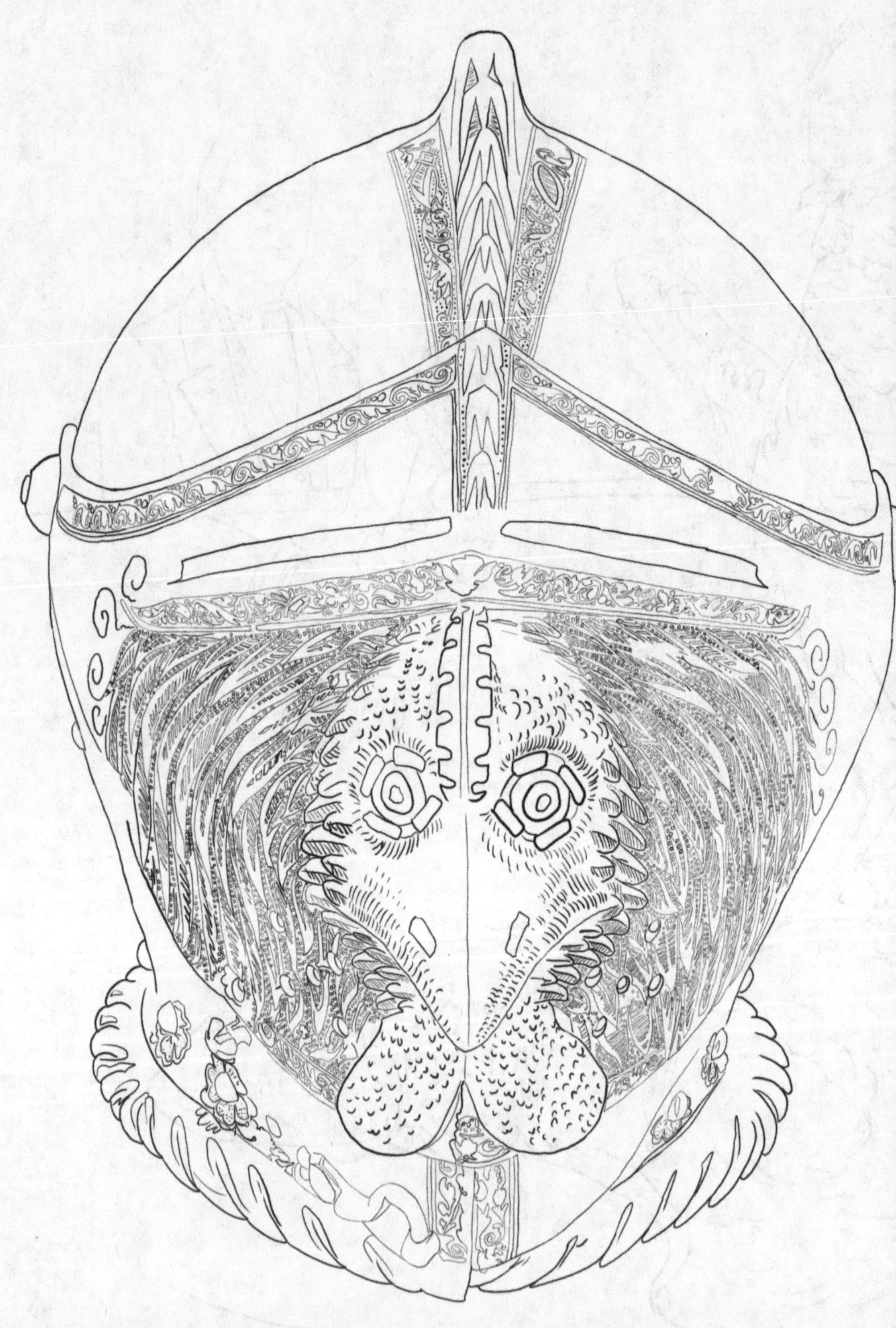

The Met Museum
Title: Armet with Mask Visor in the Form of a Rooster
Arisit: Unknown, probably form Augsburg, Germany ca. 1530
Medium: Steel

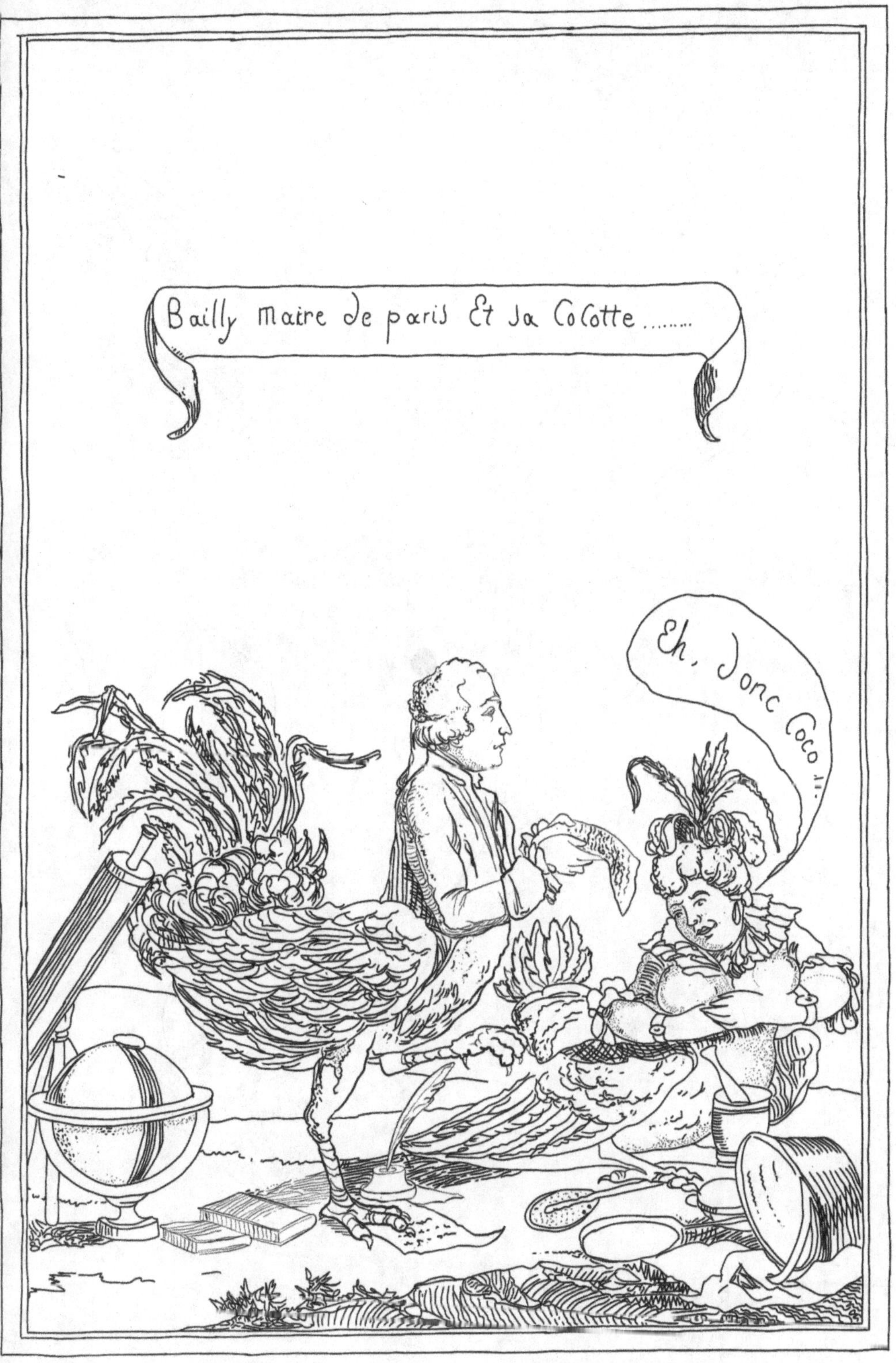

Wellcome Collection
Title: Jean Sylvain Bailly, Mayor of Paris, with his mistress, both represented as chickens.
Artist: Unknown, France 1791
Medium: Etching

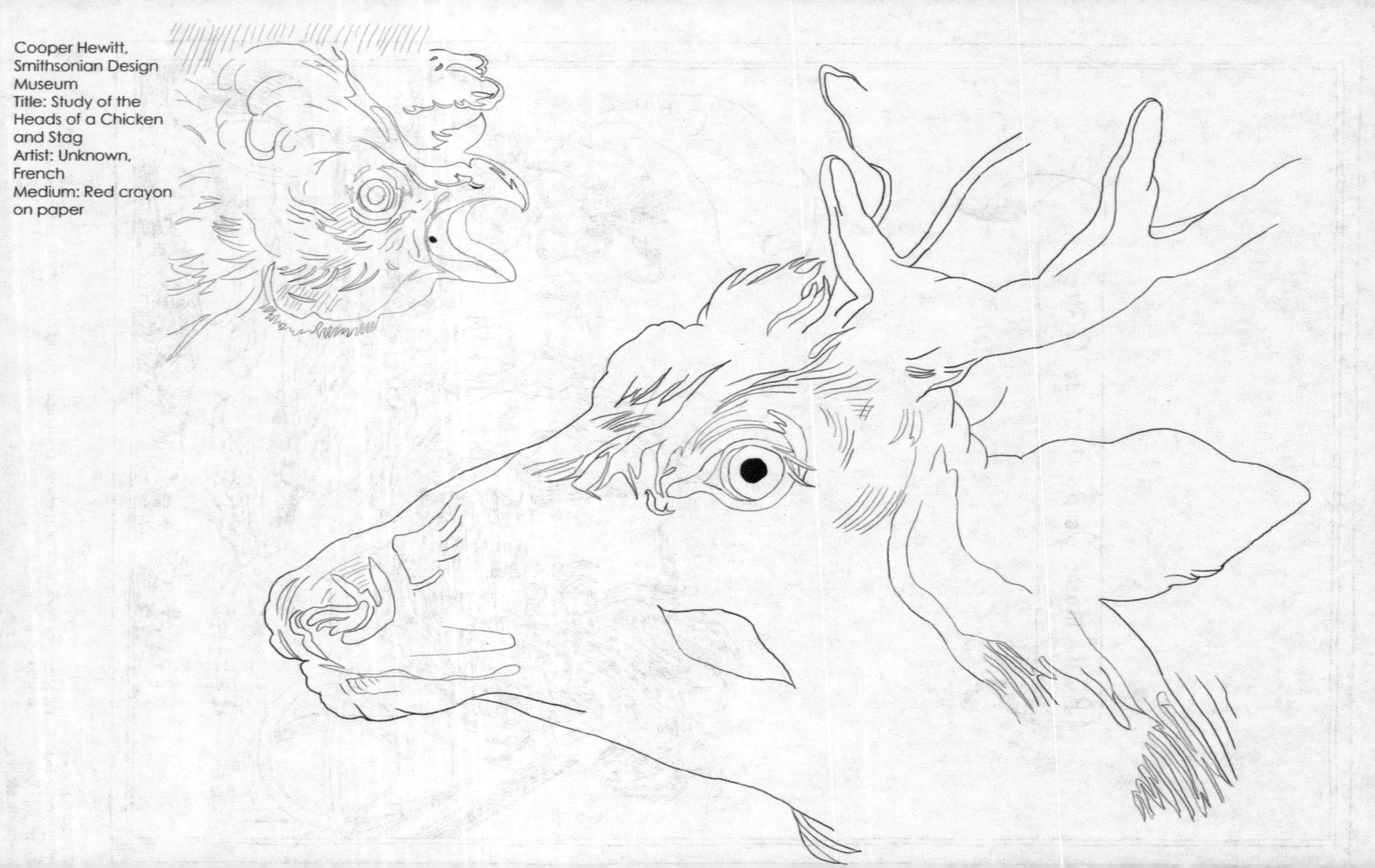

Cooper Hewitt,
Smithsonian Design
Museum
Title: Study of the
Heads of a Chicken
and Stag
Artist: Unknown,
French
Medium: Red crayon
on paper

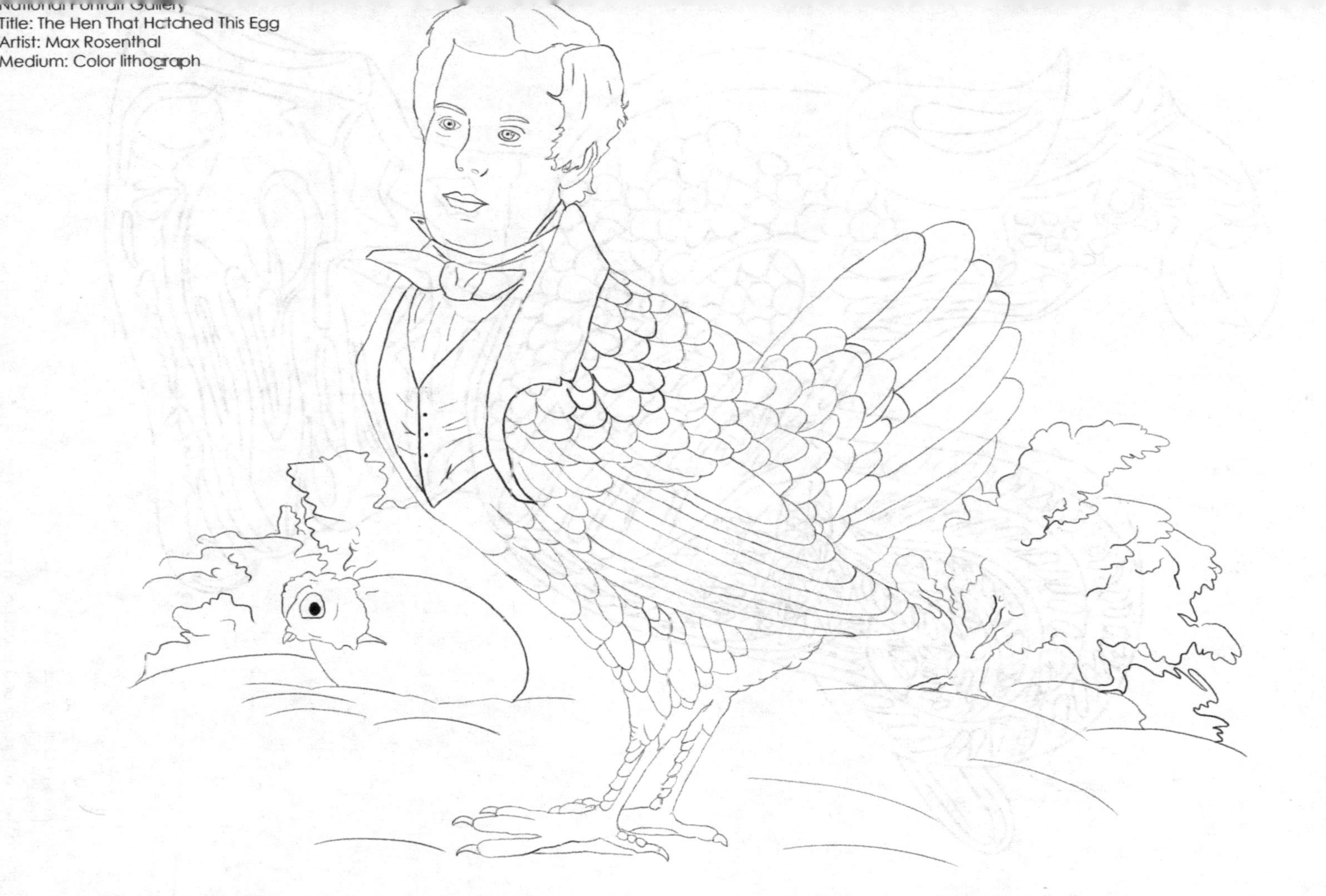

National Portrait Gallery
Title: The Hen That Hatched This Egg
Artist: Max Rosenthal
Medium: Color lithograph

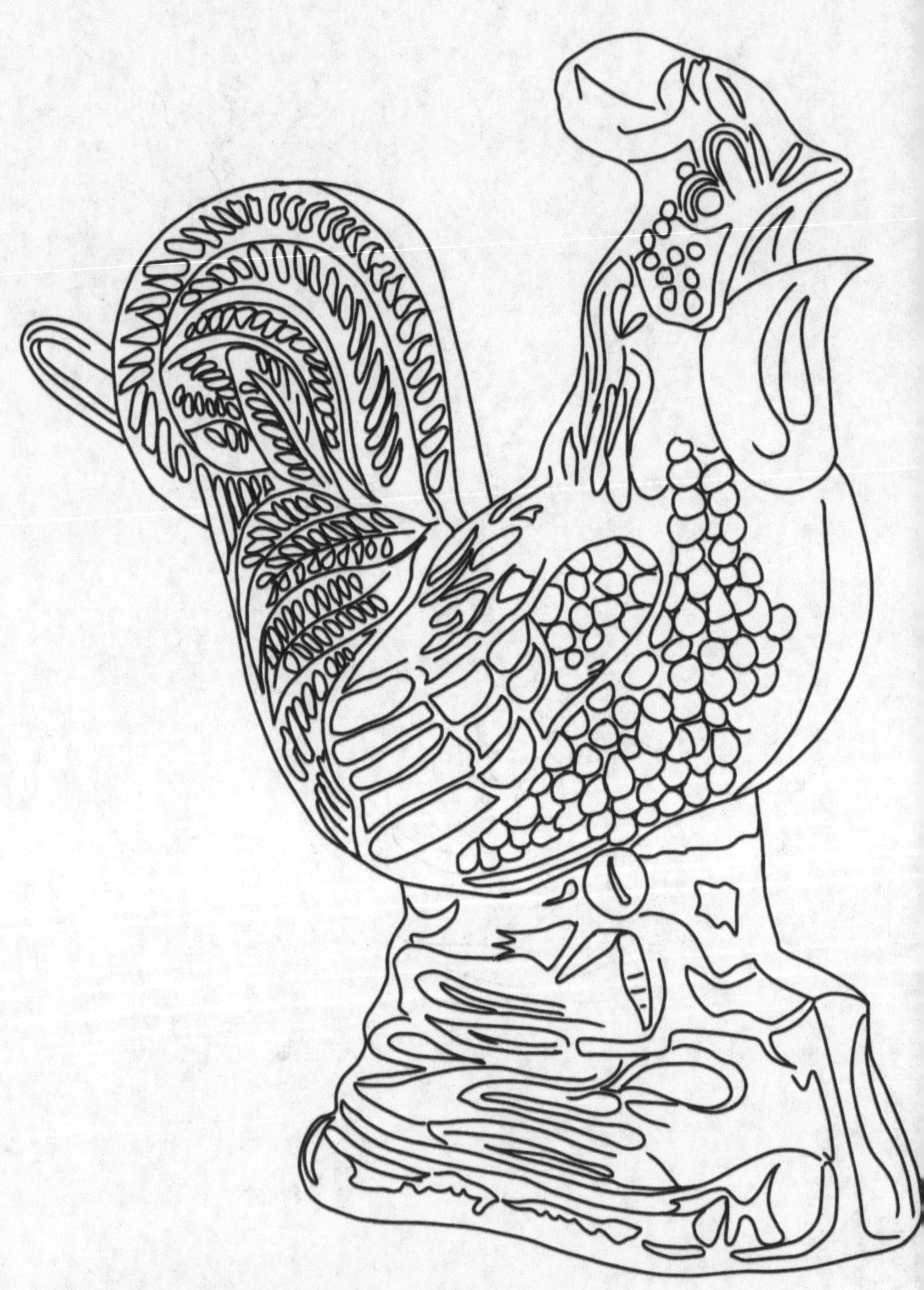

National Gallery of Art
Title: Rooster Coin Bank, c. 1938
Artist: William O. Fletcher
Medium: Watercolor and gouache on paper

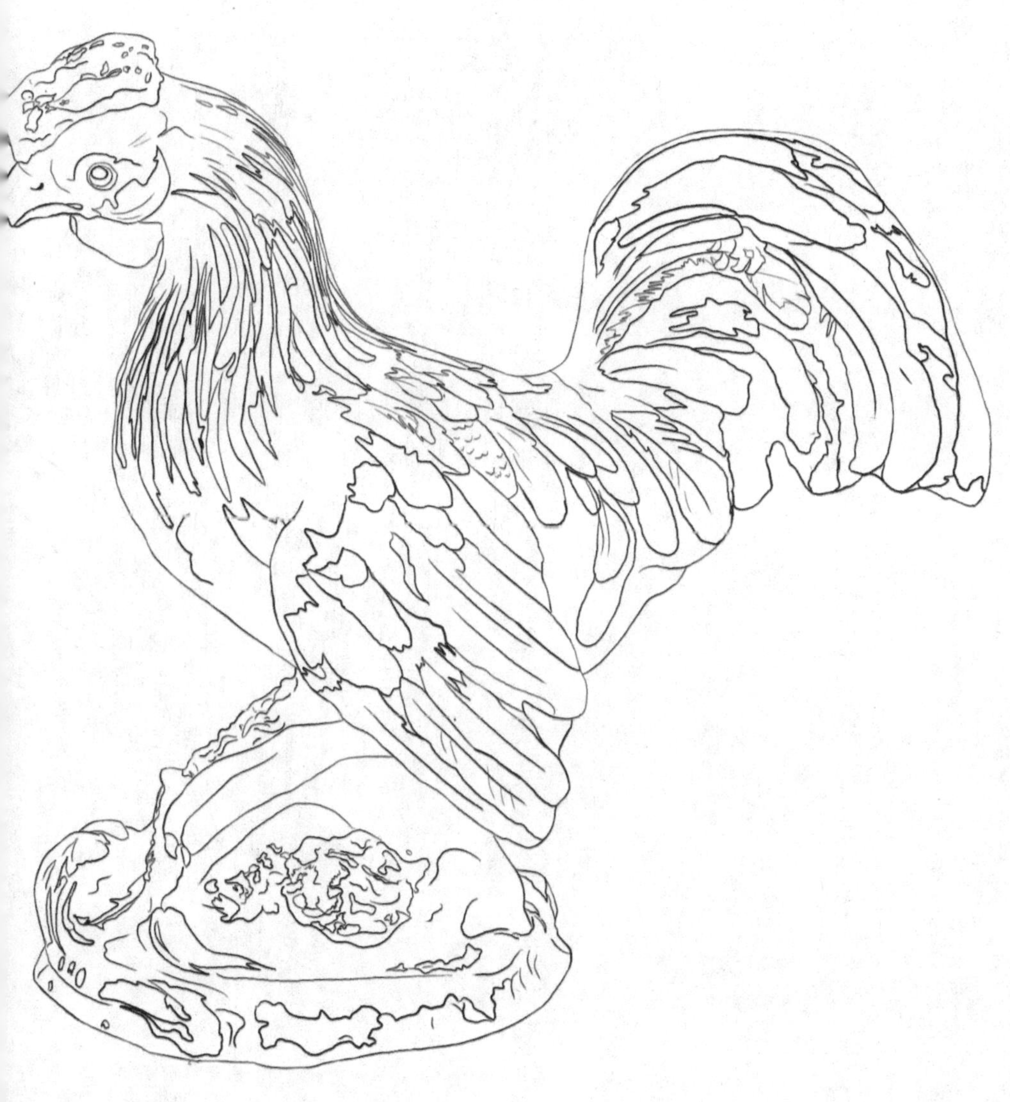

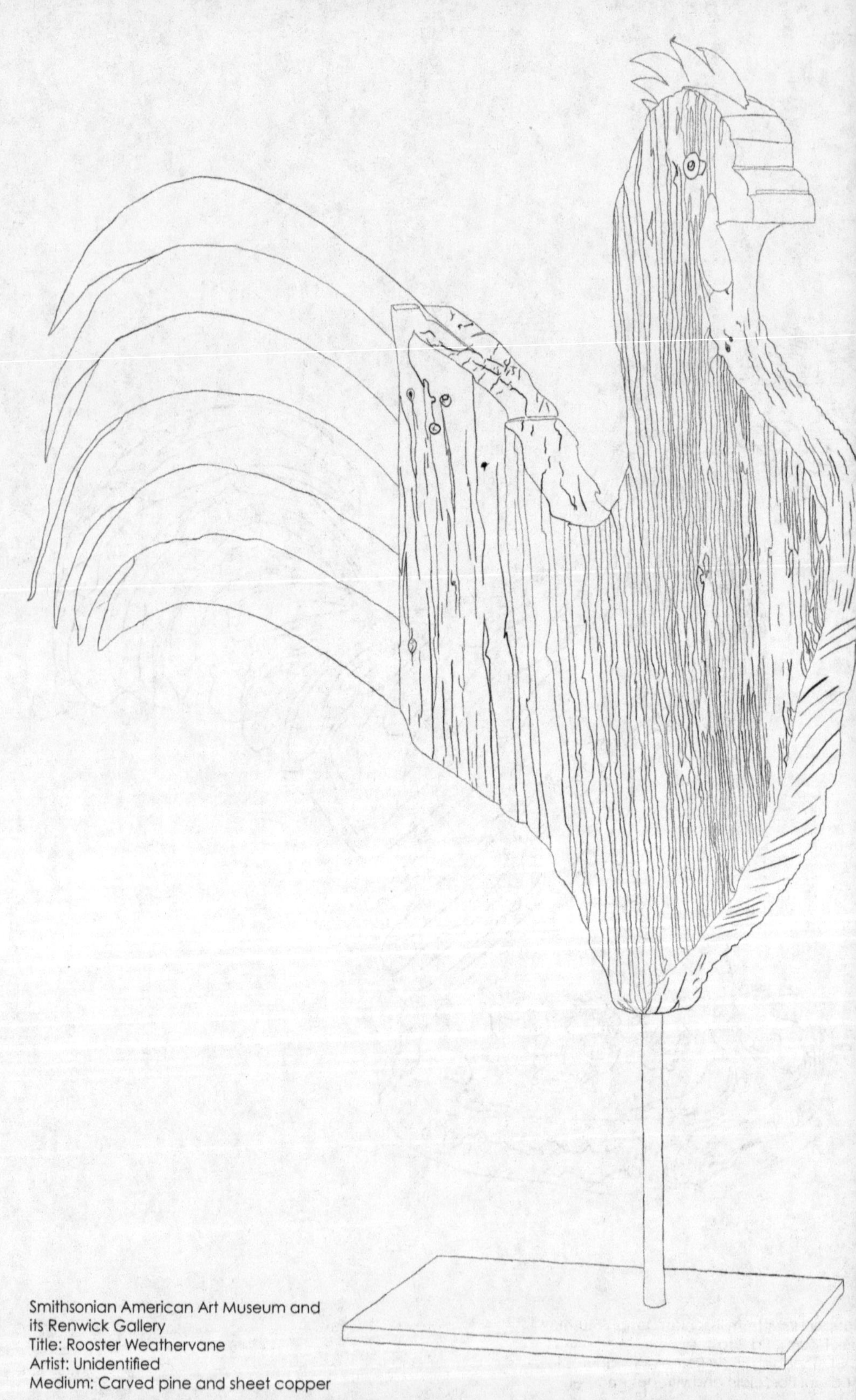

Smithsonian American Art Museum and
its Renwick Gallery
Title: Rooster Weathervane
Artist: Unidentified
Medium: Carved pine and sheet copper

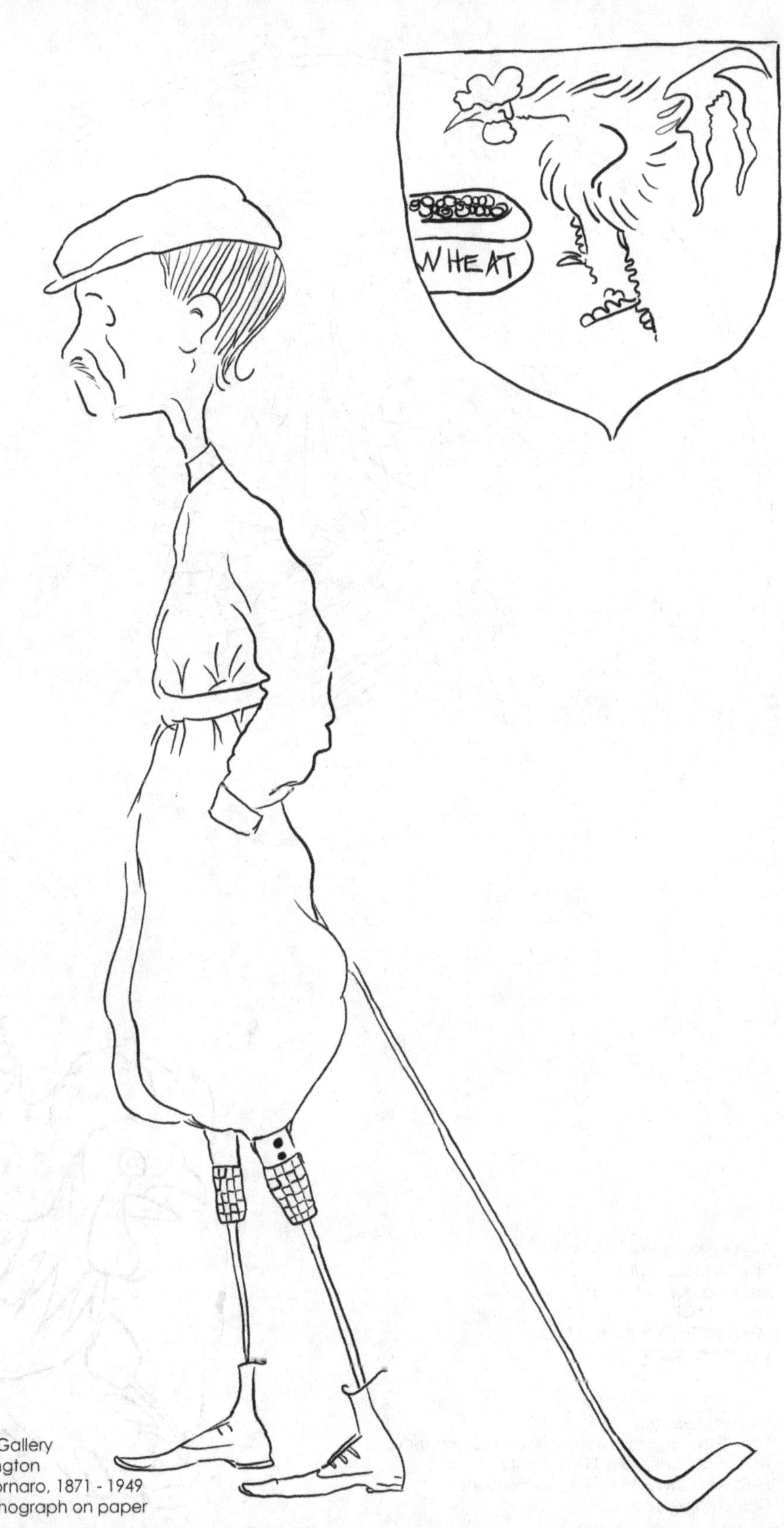

National Portrait Gallery
Title: E. C. Worthington
Artist: Carlo de Fornaro, 1871 - 1949
Medium: Color lithograph on paper

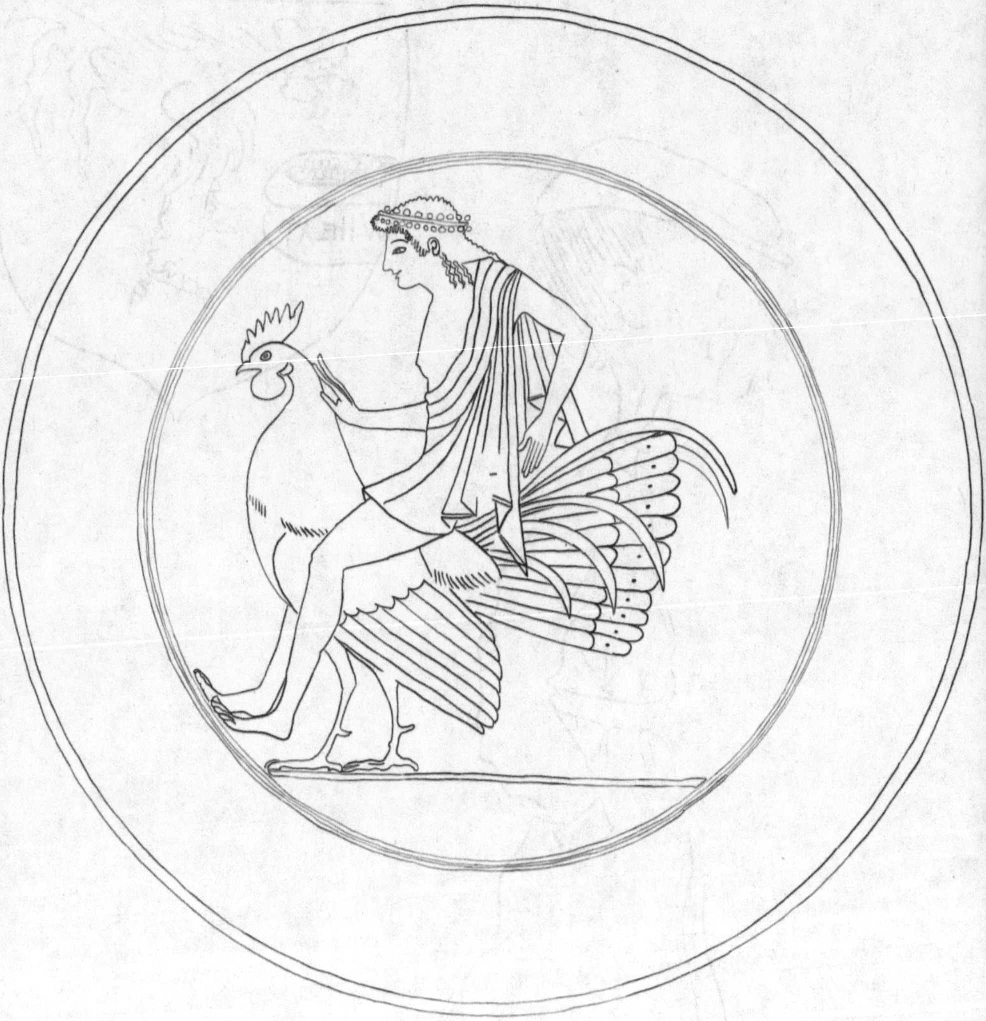

The Met Museum
Title: Terracotta plate
Artist: Signed by Epiktetos as painter, ca.
520–510 BCE
Medium: Terracotta; red-figure
Depicted above

The Met Museum
Title: "Rooster", Folio from a dispersed Manuscript
Artist: Unknown, 10th-11th century
Medium: Opaque water color on paper
Depicted right

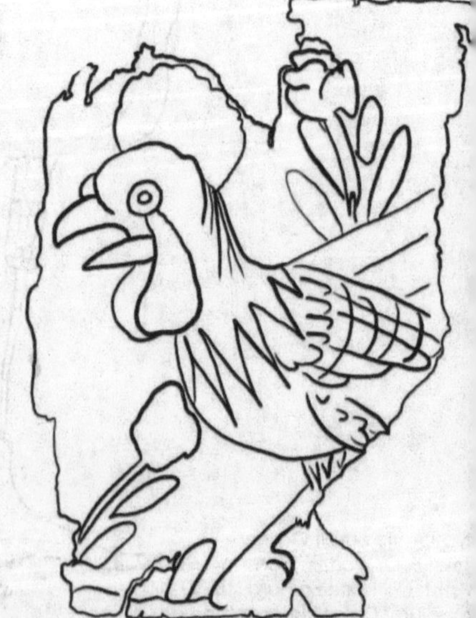

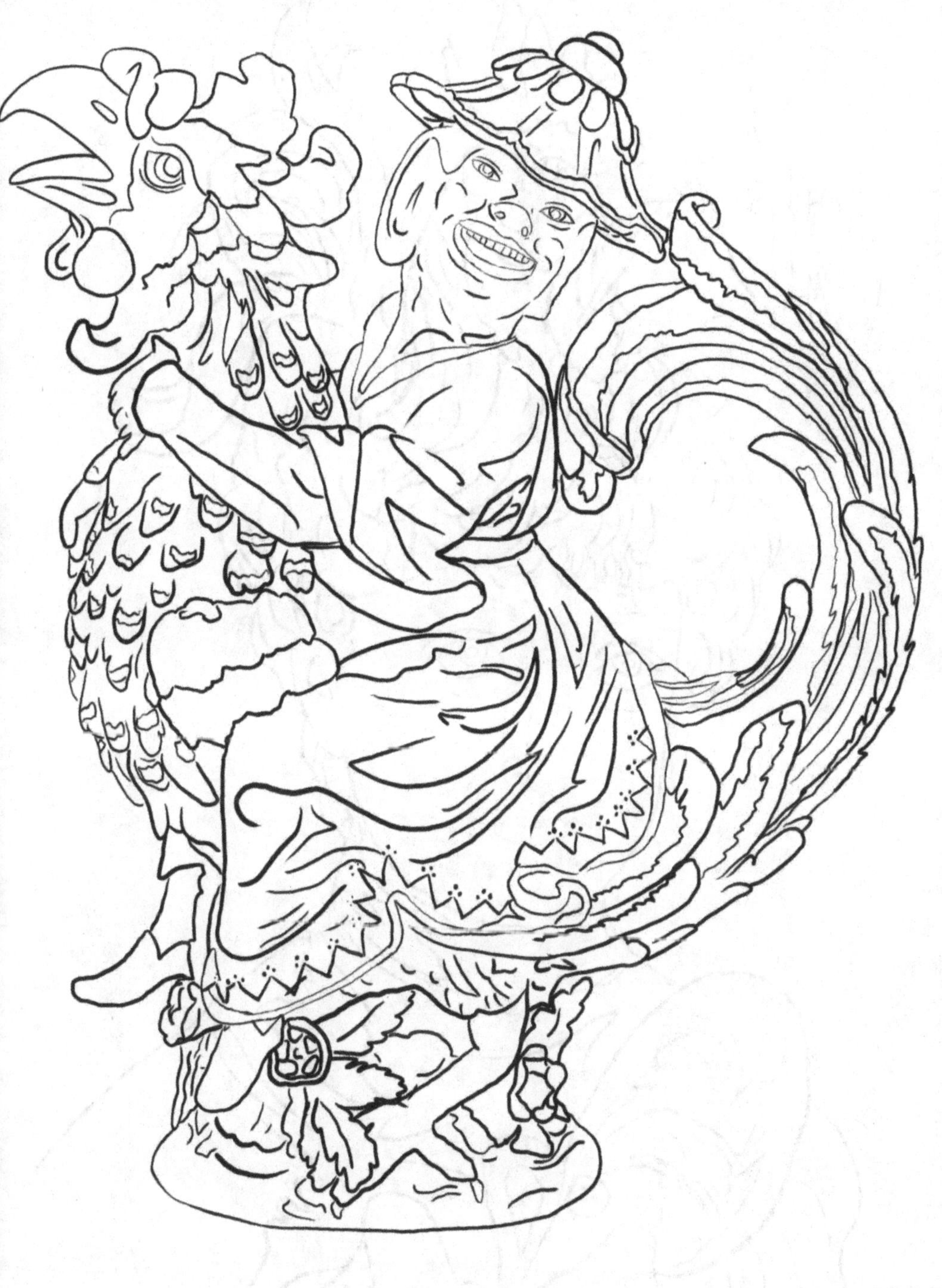

The Met Museum
Title: Oil of vinegar cruet
Artist: Johann Joachim Kändler/ Meissen Manufactory
Medium: Hard-paste porcelain

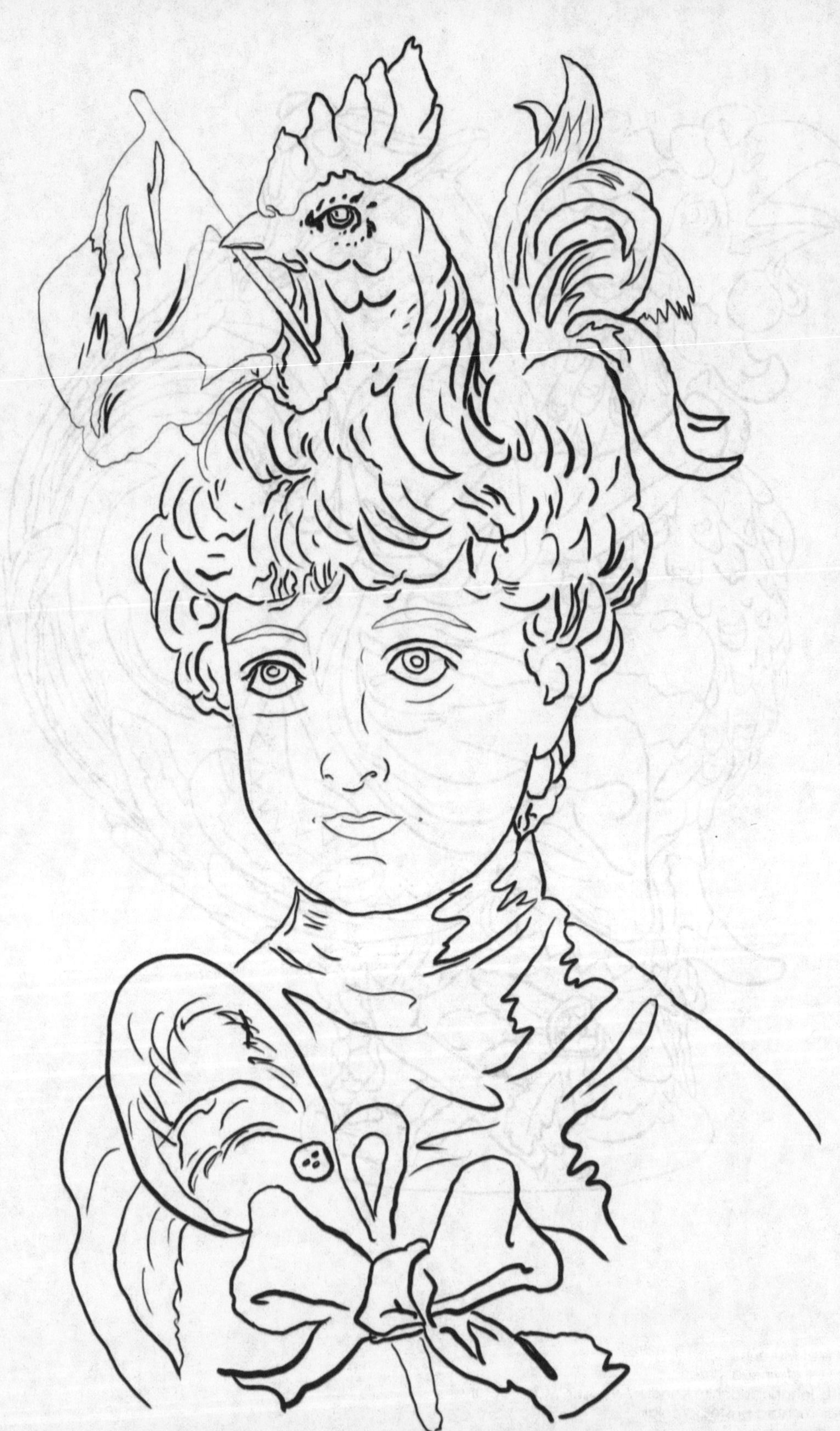

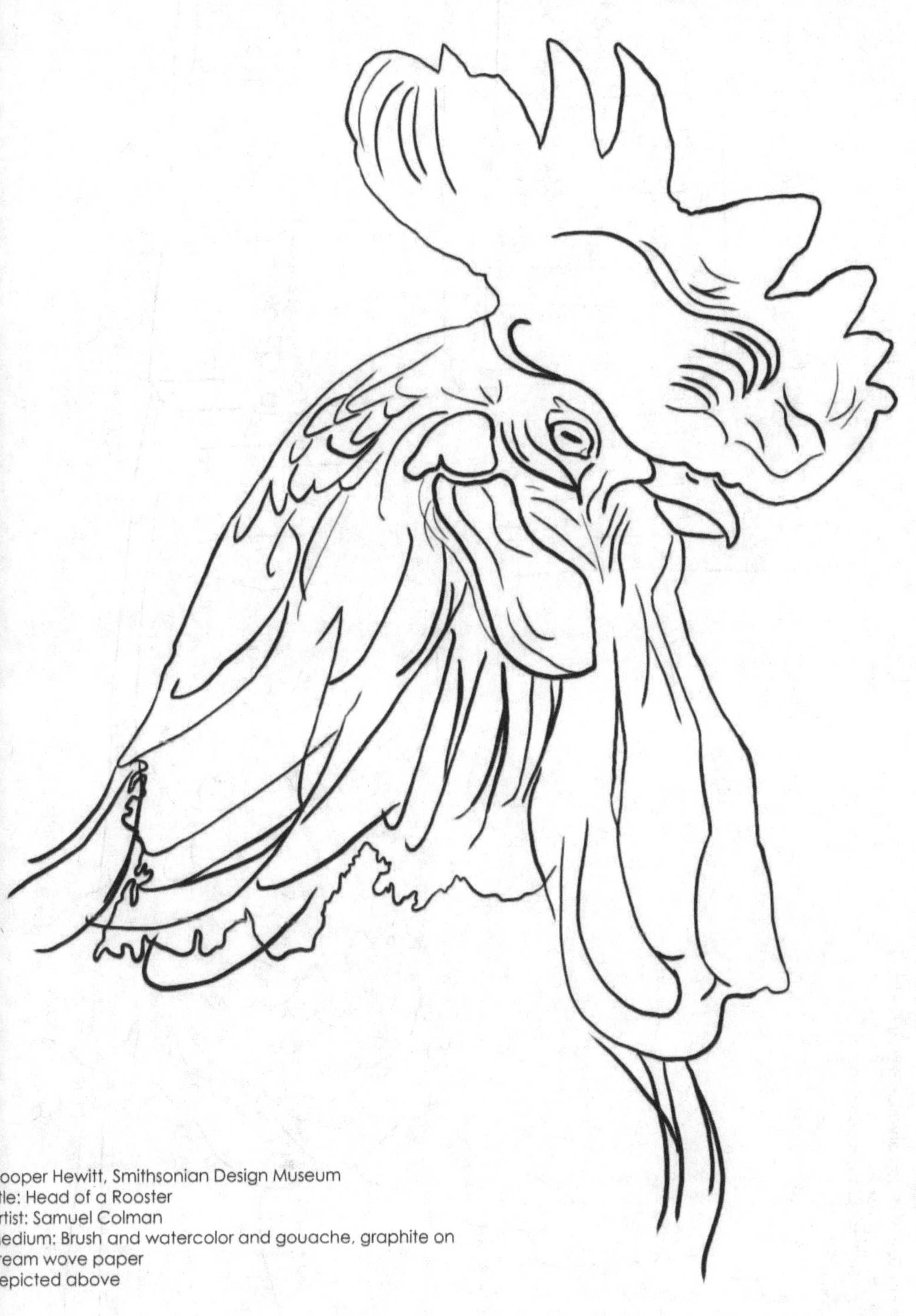

ooper Hewitt, Smithsonian Design Museum
tle: Head of a Rooster
rtist: Samuel Colman
edium: Brush and watercolor and gouache, graphite on
eam wove paper
epicted above

ne Met Museum
tle: Maud Harrison as "The Chanticleer," from the series Fancy Dress Ball
Costumes (N73) for Duke brand cigarettes
rtist: W. Duke, Sons & Co. (New York and Durham, N.C.) 1889
Medium: Commercial color lithograph
epicted left

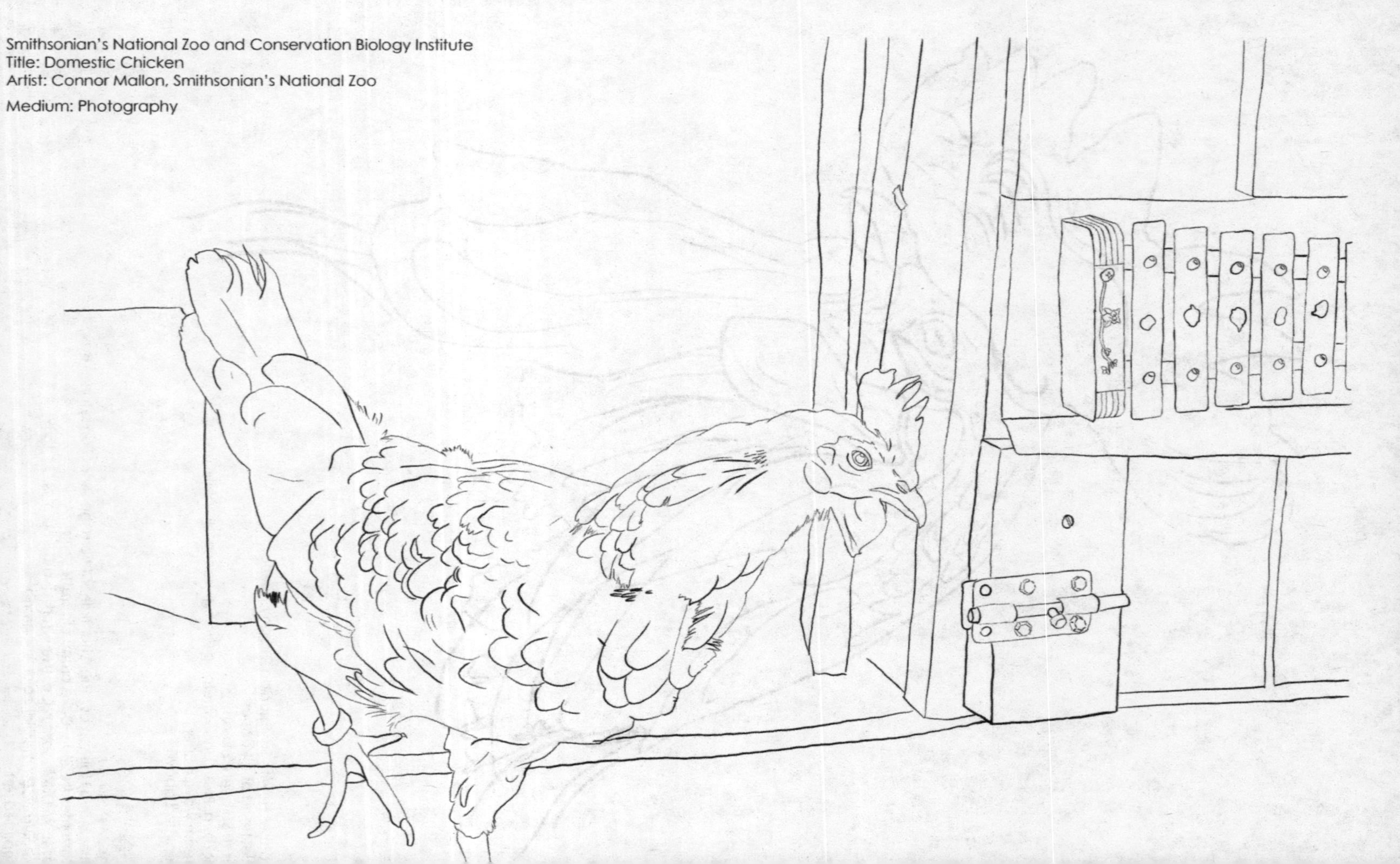

Smithsonian's National Zoo and Conservation Biology Institute
Title: Domestic Chicken
Artist: Connor Mallon, Smithsonian's National Zoo
Medium: Photography

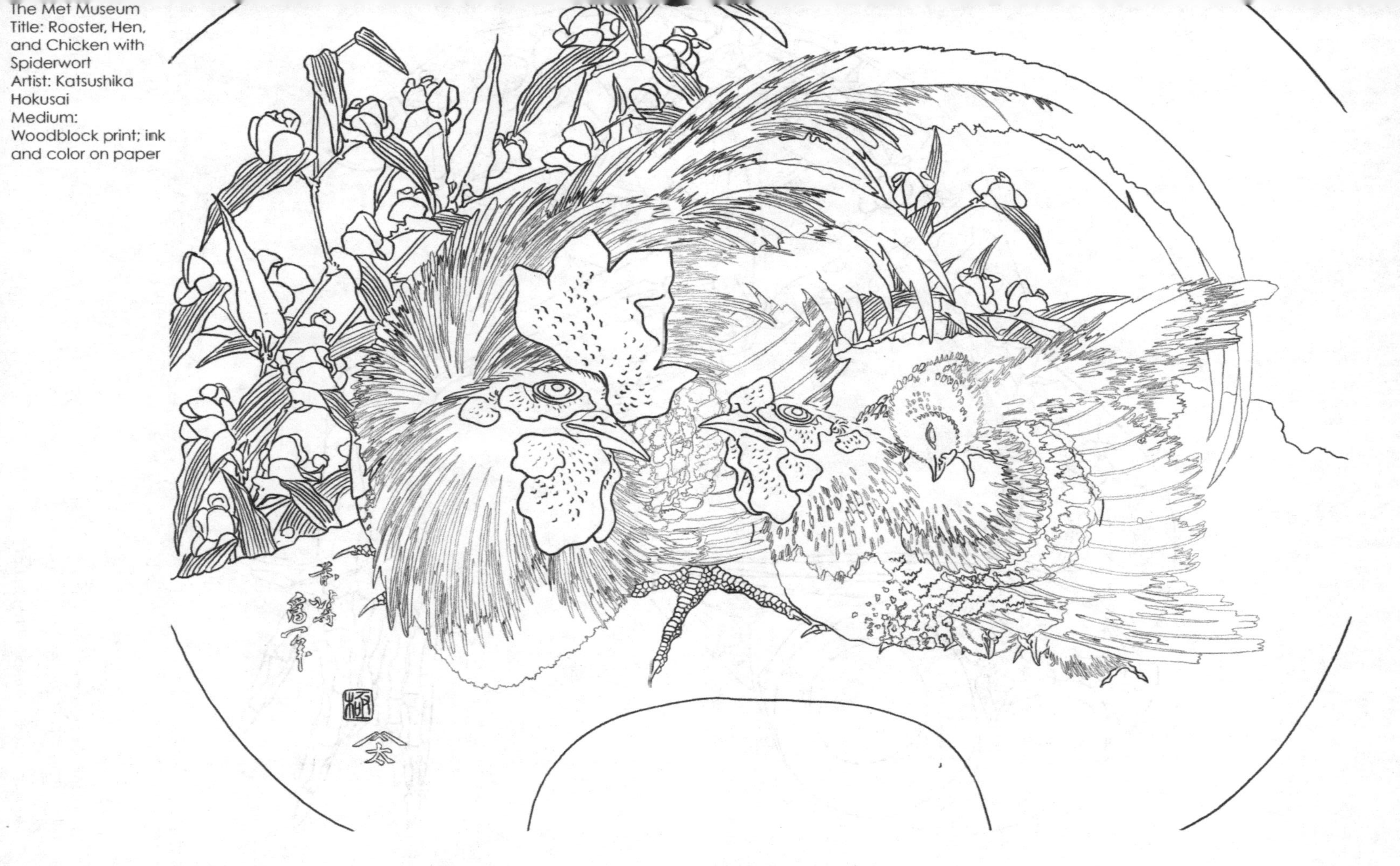

The Met Museum
Title: Rooster, Hen, and Chicken with Spiderwort
Artist: Katsushika Hokusai
Medium: Woodblock print; ink and color on paper

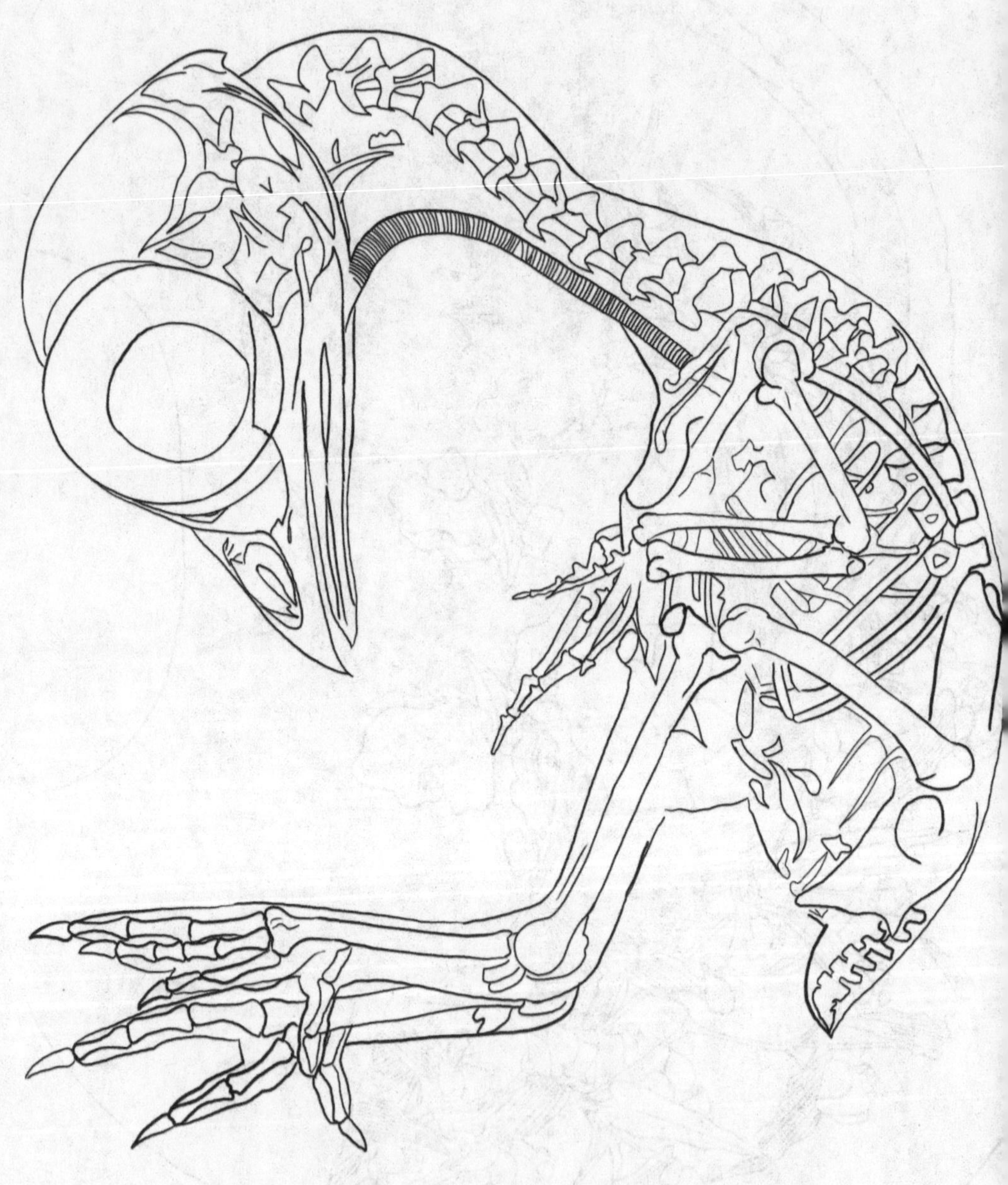

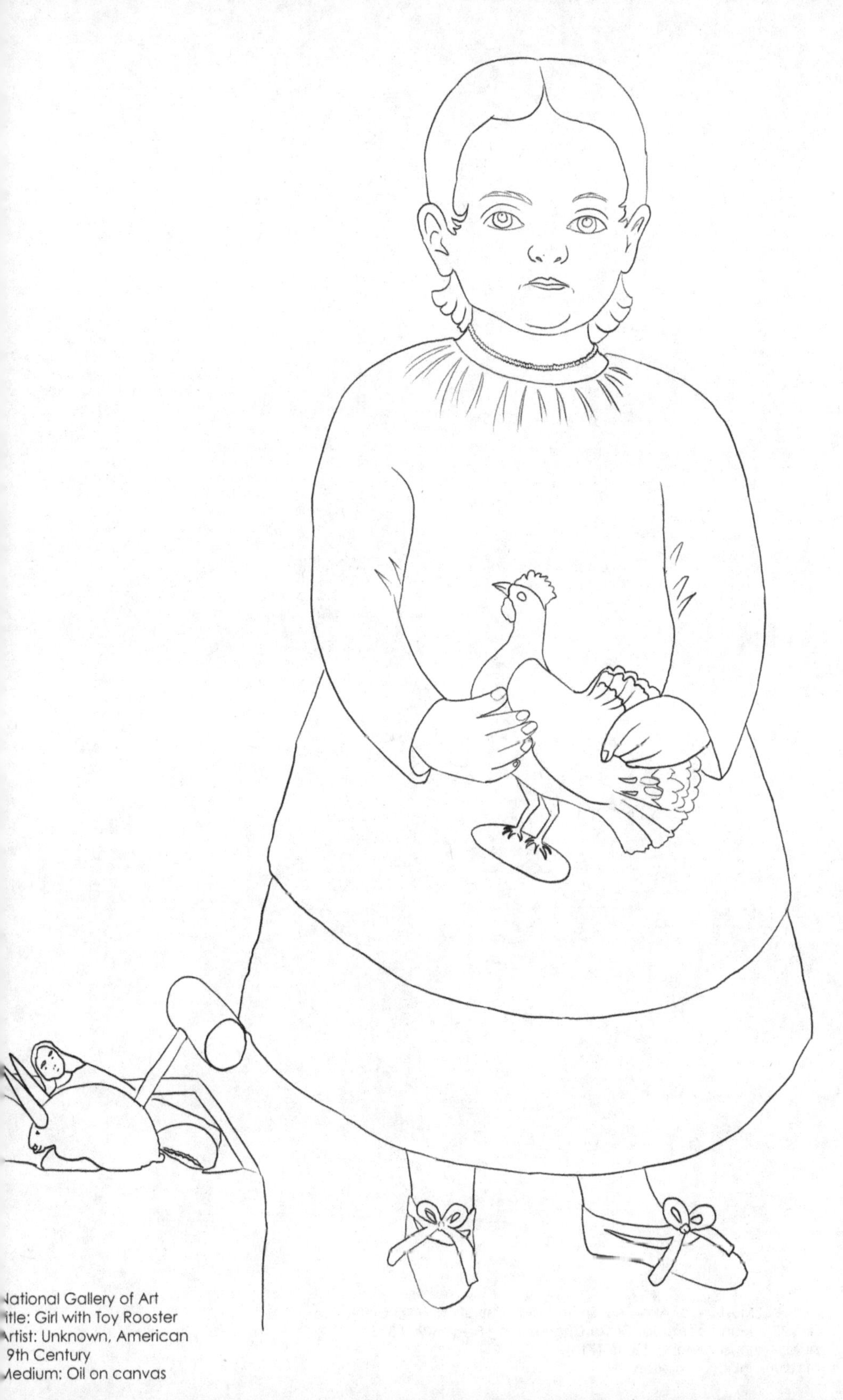

National Gallery of Art
Title: Girl with Toy Rooster
Artist: Unknown, American
19th Century
Medium: Oil on canvas

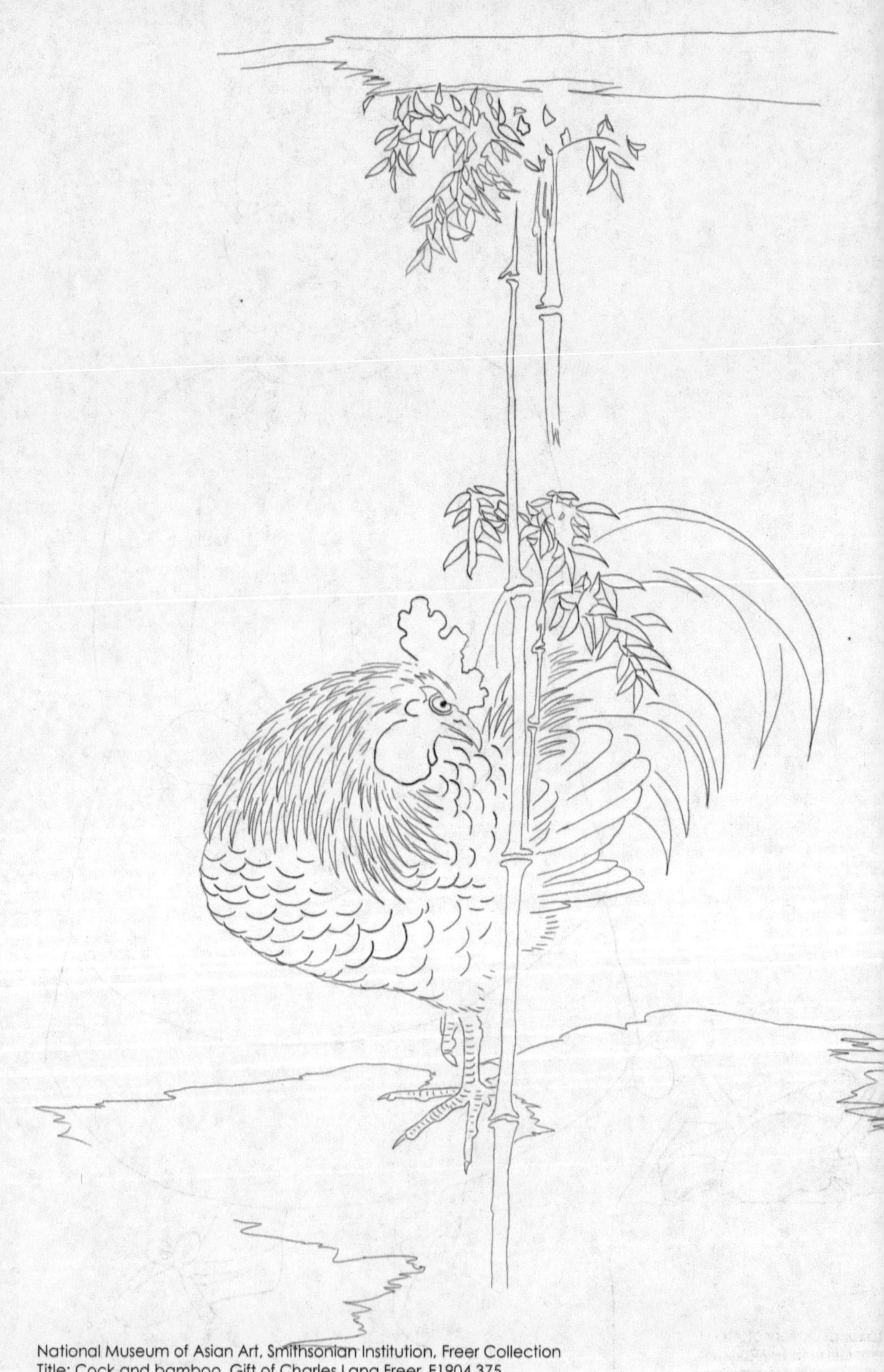

National Museum of Asian Art, Smithsonian Institution, Freer Collection
Title: Cock and bamboo, Gift of Charles Lang Freer, F1904.375
Artist: Kano Tsunenobu (1636-1713)
Medium: Ink and color on silk

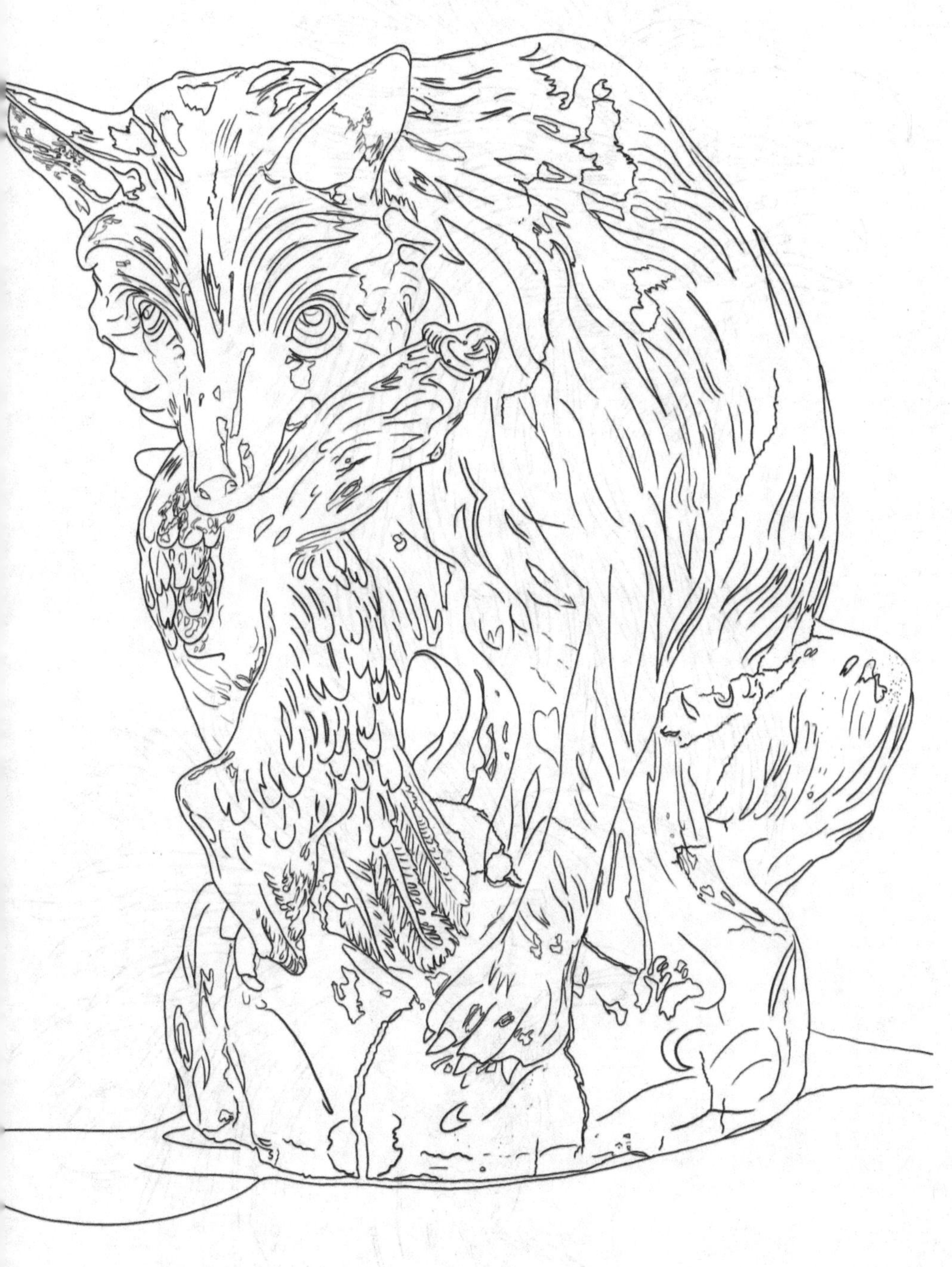

Title: A Fox with a Chicken
Artist: Johann Gottlieb Kirchner
Medium: Porcelain

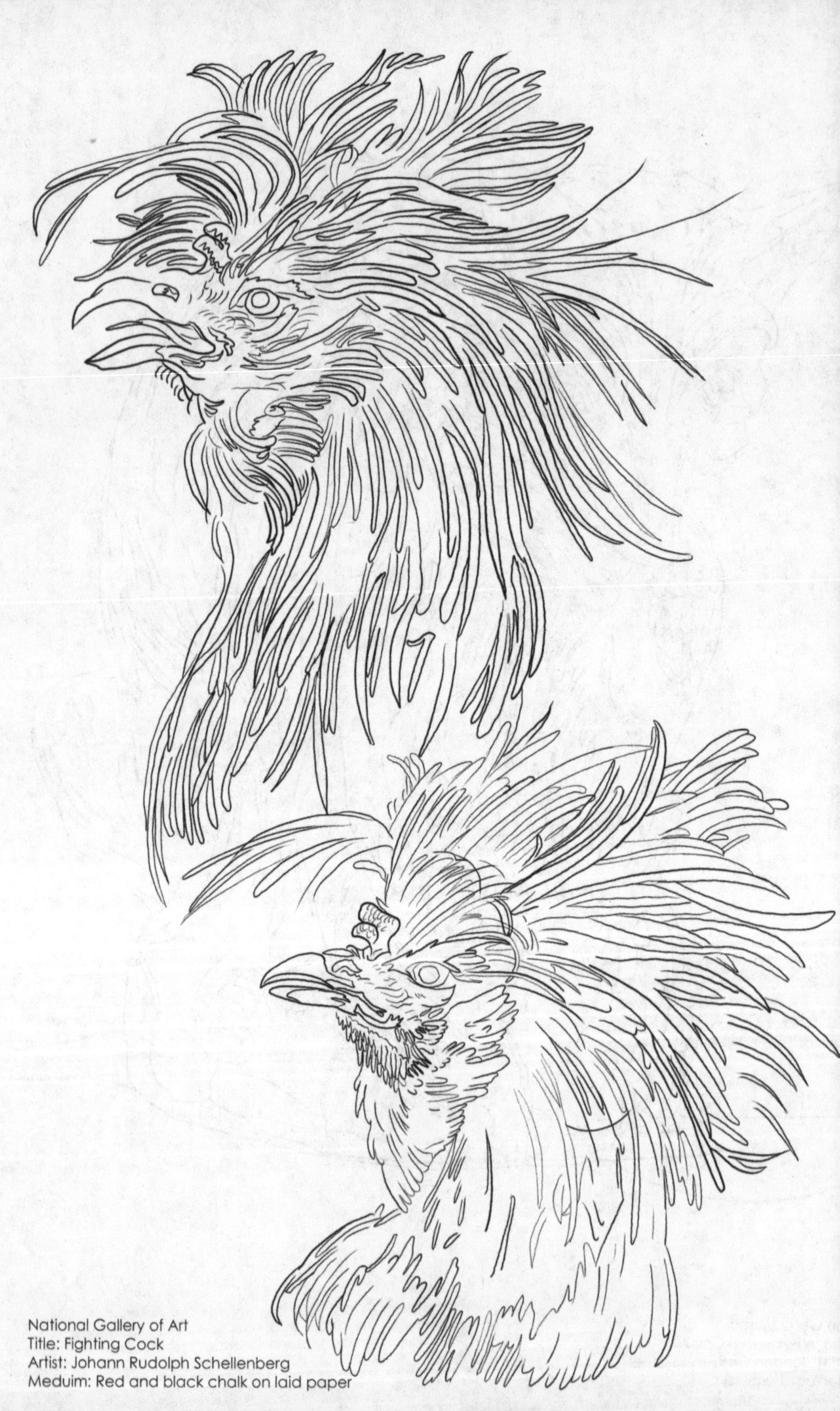

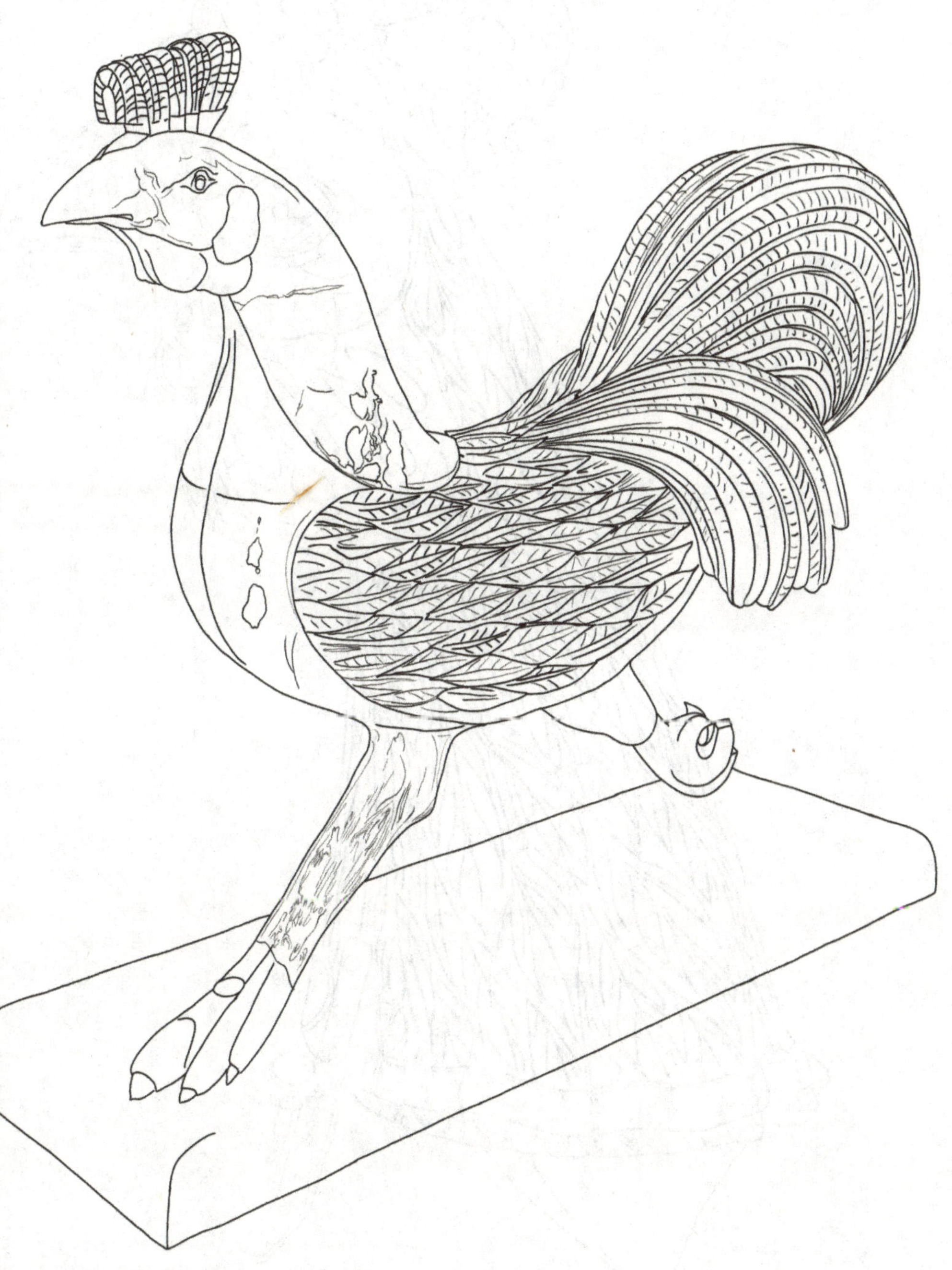

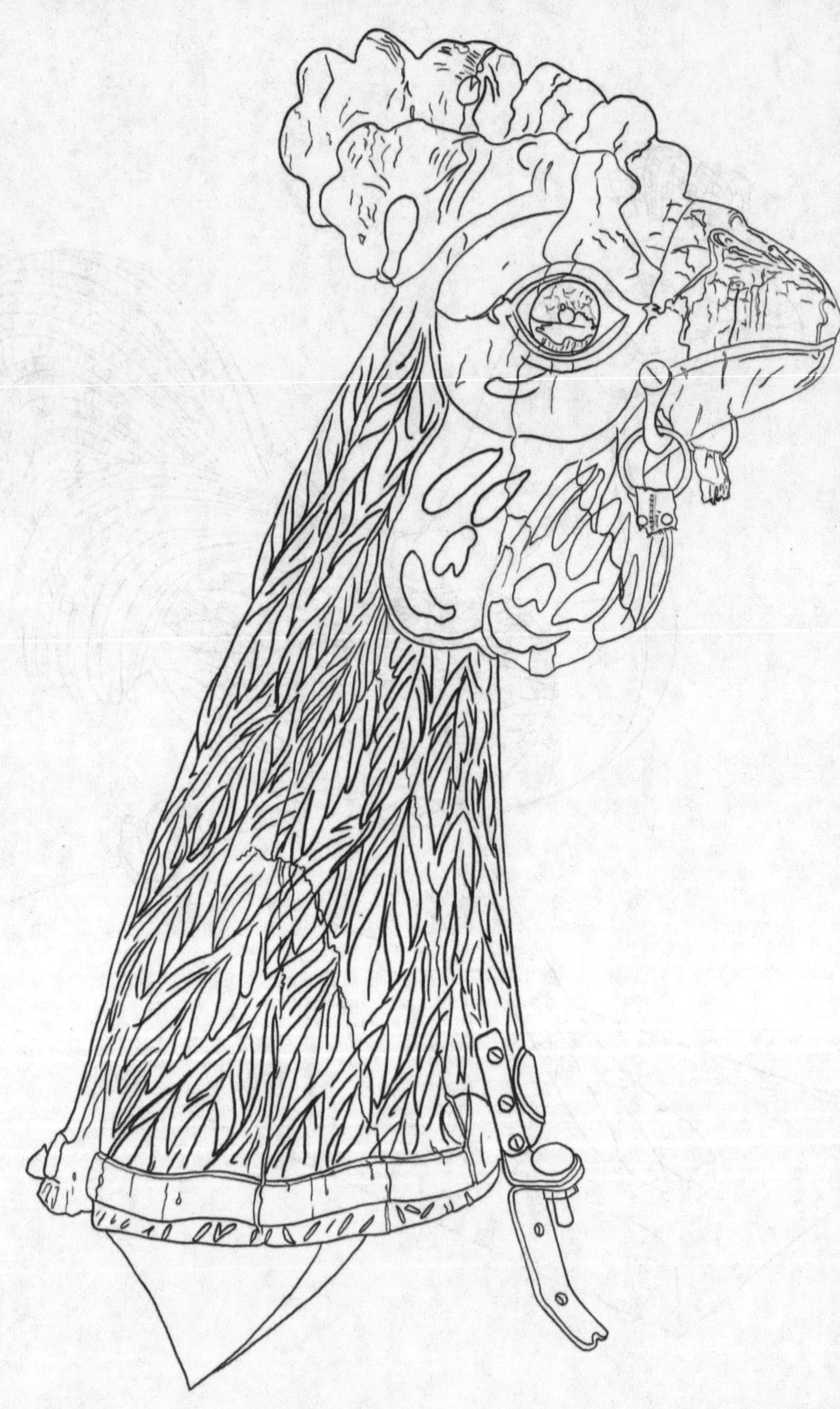

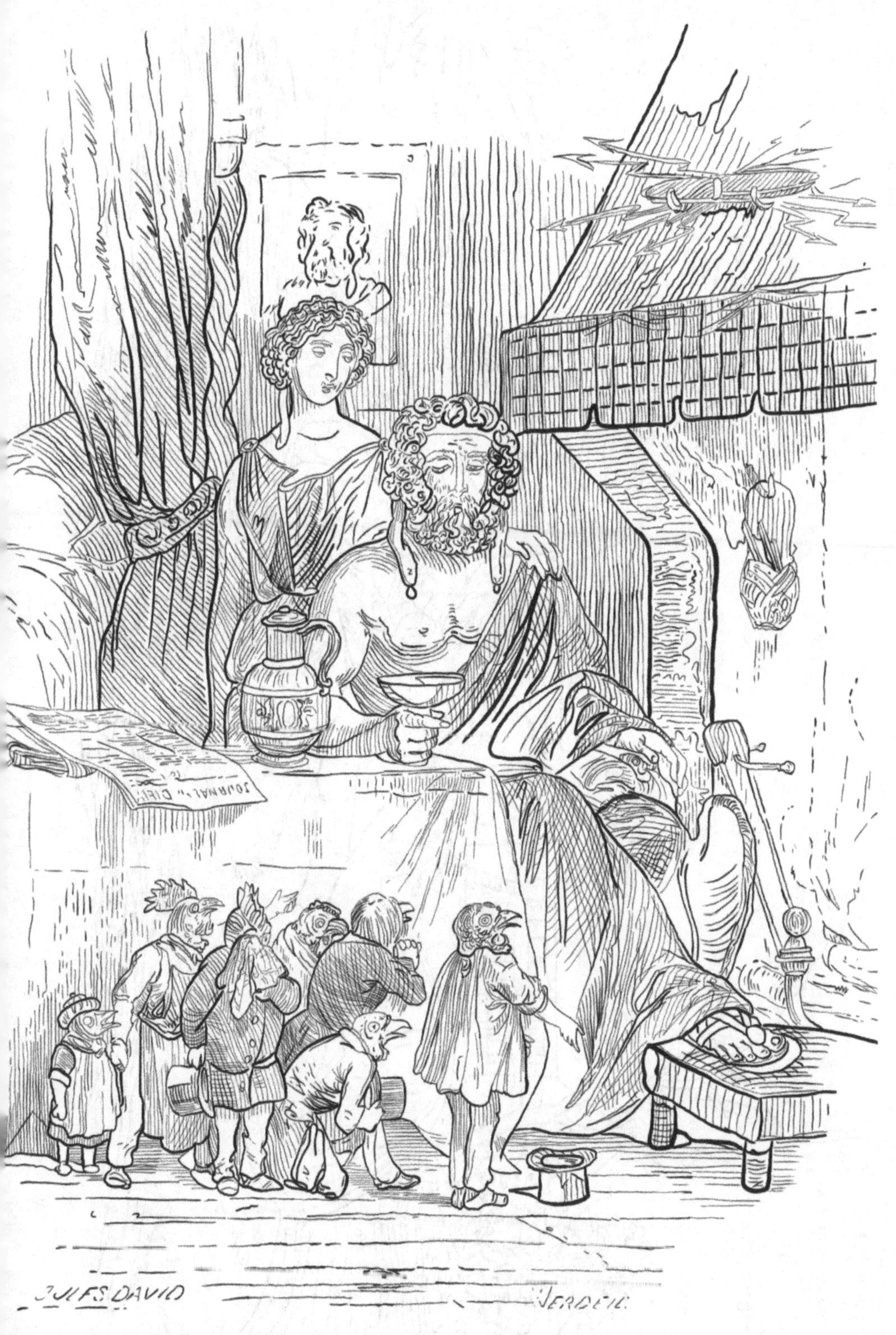

The Met Museum
Title: Jupiter and the Chickens (Jupiter et les Poulets)
Artist: After Jules David/ Pierre Verdeil
Medium: Wood Engraving

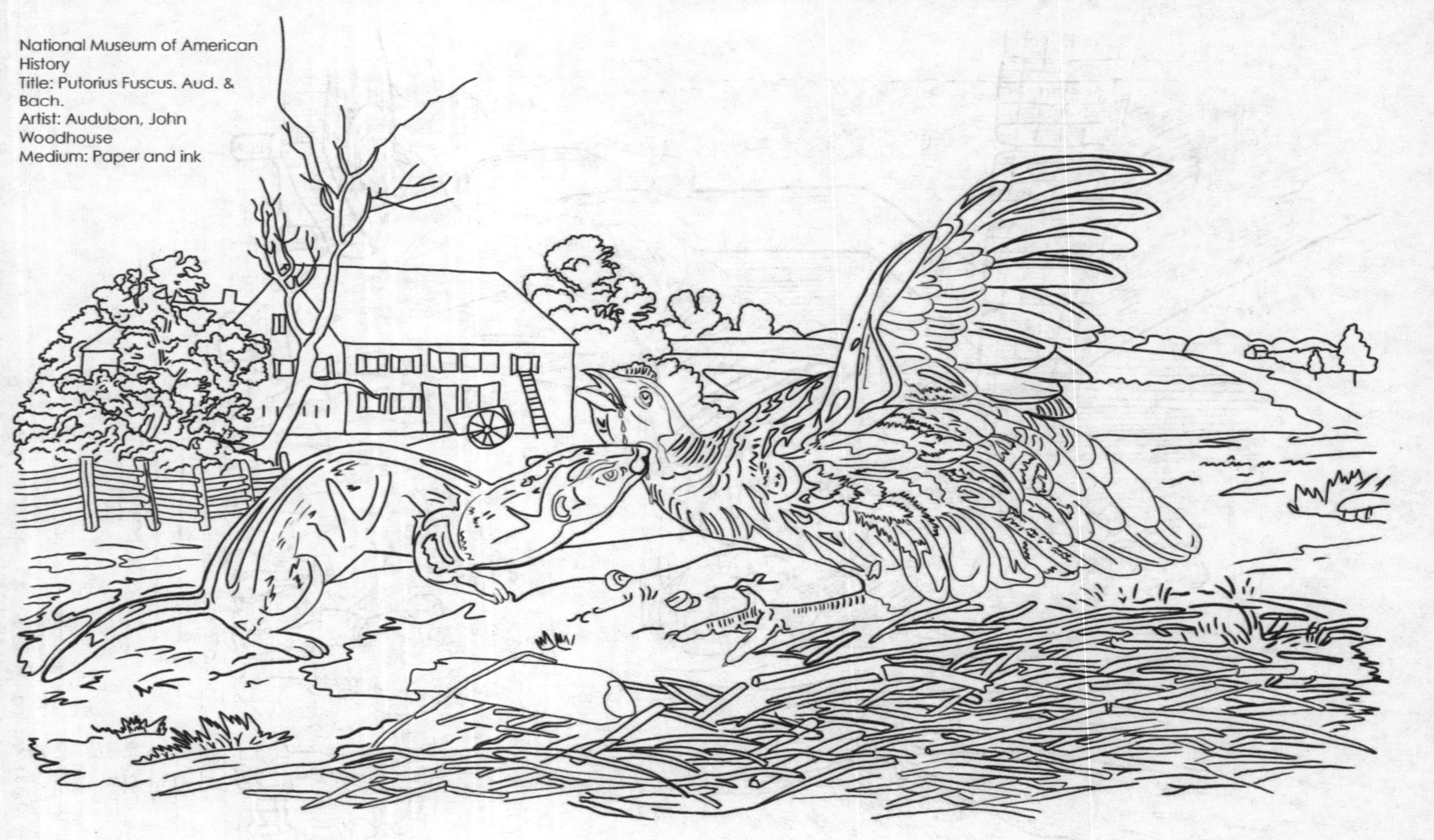

National Museum of American History
Title: Putorius Fuscus. Aud. & Bach.
Artist: Audubon, John Woodhouse
Medium: Paper and ink

Title: A Cat and A Sitting Hen
Artist: Agosto Carracci (allegedly)
Meduim: Pen and brown ink on paper

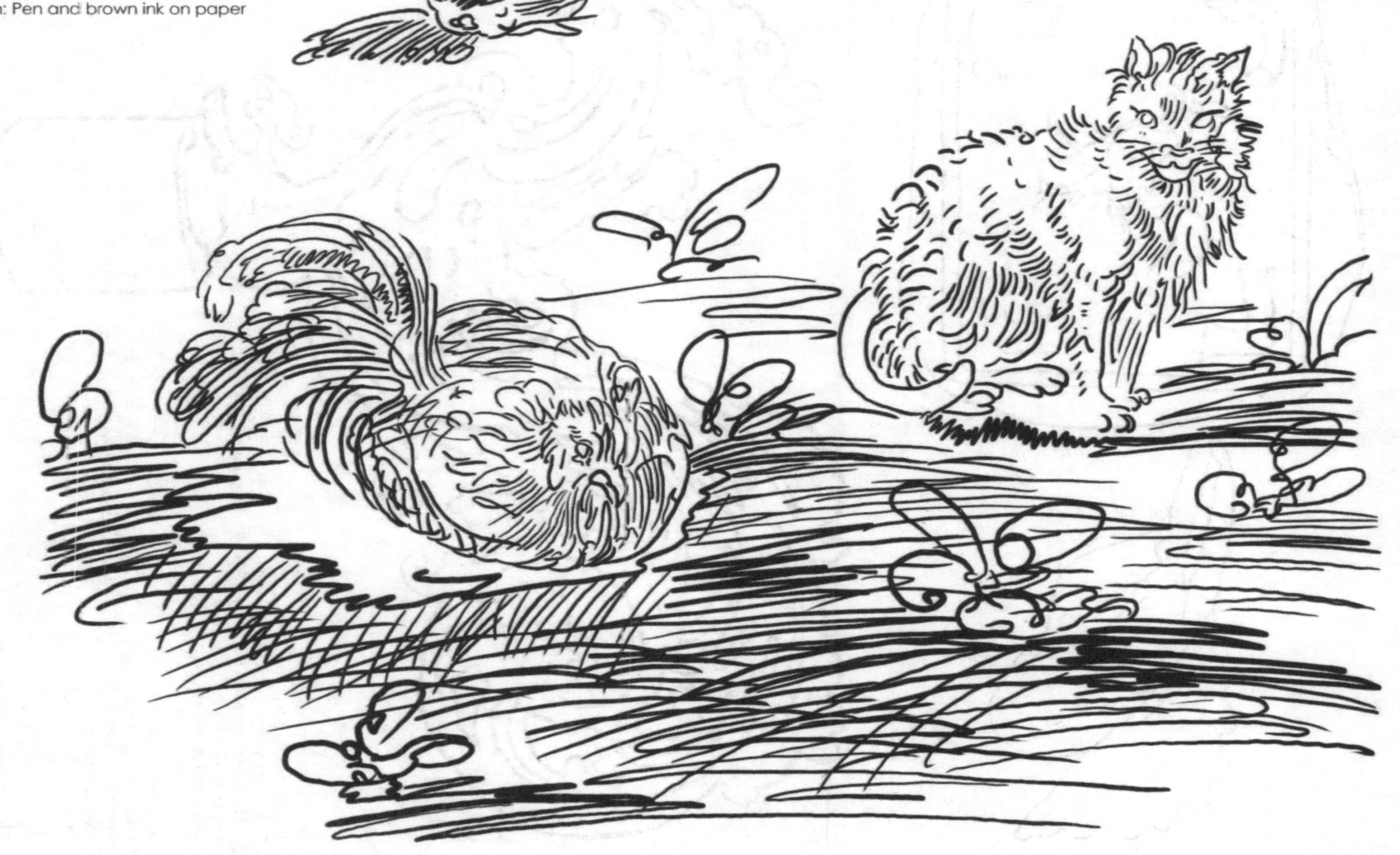

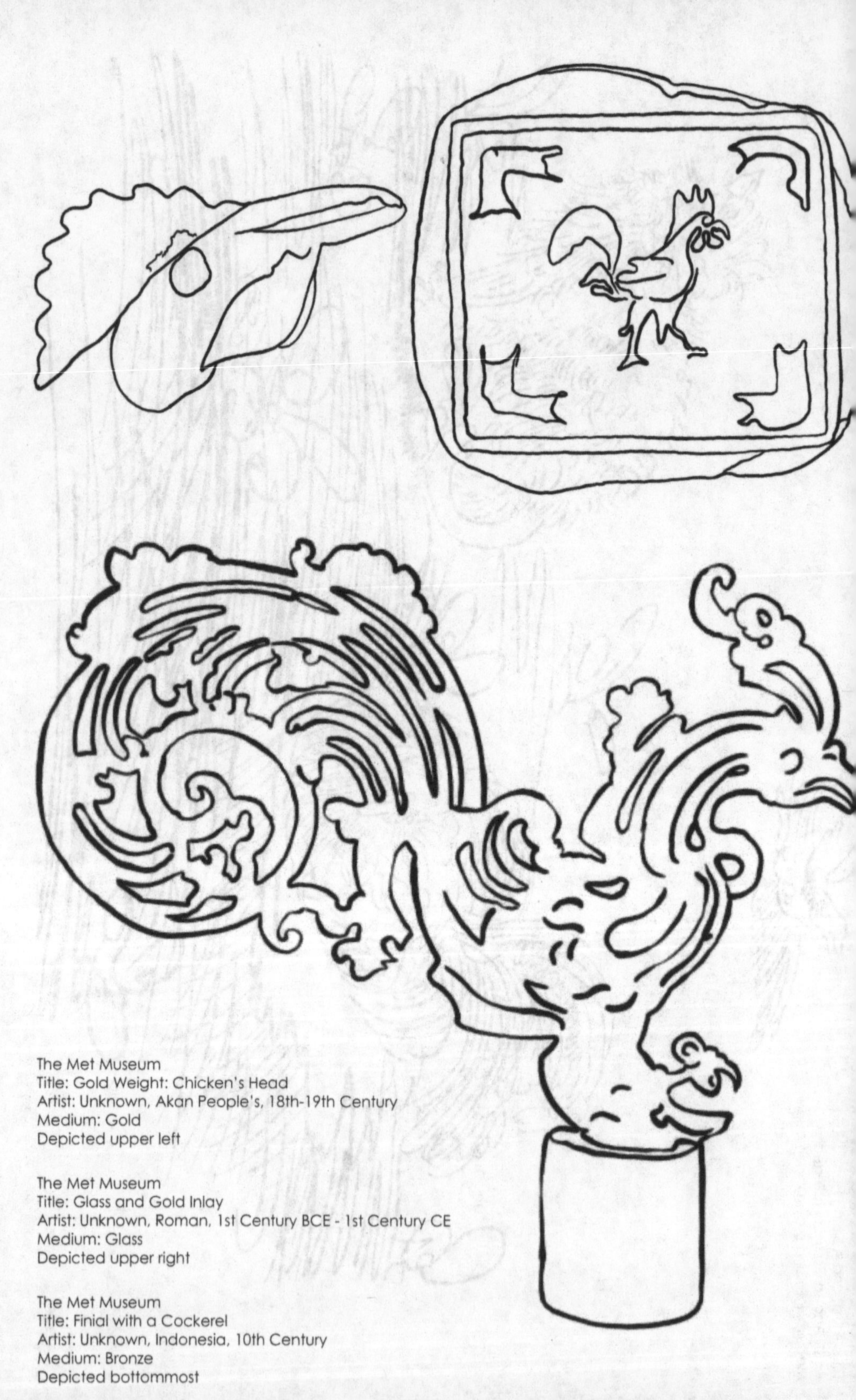

The Met Museum
Title: Gold Weight: Chicken's Head
Artist: Unknown, Akan People's, 18th-19th Century
Medium: Gold
Depicted upper left

The Met Museum
Title: Glass and Gold Inlay
Artist: Unknown, Roman, 1st Century BCE - 1st Century CE
Medium: Glass
Depicted upper right

The Met Museum
Title: Finial with a Cockerel
Artist: Unknown, Indonesia, 10th Century
Medium: Bronze
Depicted bottommost

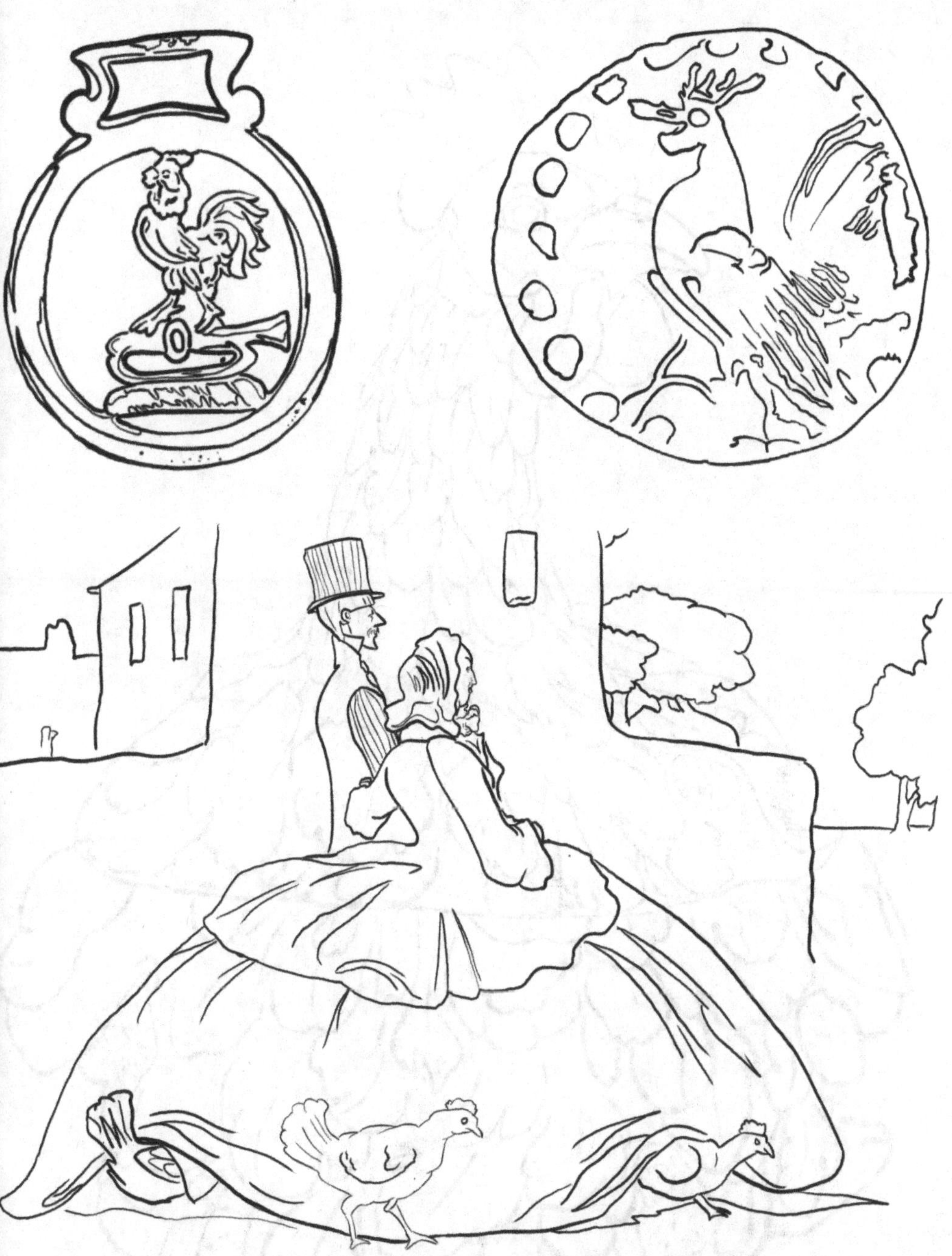

The Art Institute Chicago
Title: An Excusable Error. Chickens thinking they have found the cage where they spent their early childhood, plate 21 from La Crinolomanie
Artist: Honoré Victorin Daumier
Medium: Lithograph in black on white wove paper
Depicted lowest

The Cleveland Museum of Art, Gift of the John Huntington Art and Polytechnic Trust 1917.989.a
Title: Drachm: Rooster (obverse), c. 530–483 BC. Artist: Unknown, Greek, minted at Himera (Sicily)
Medium: Silver; diameter: 2.1 cm (13/16 in.)
Depicted Upper right

Museums Victoria Collections
Title: Drawing of Horse Brass - Rooster, ST 34343
Artist: Unknown, England, 1825-1939
Medium: Metal
Depicted upper left

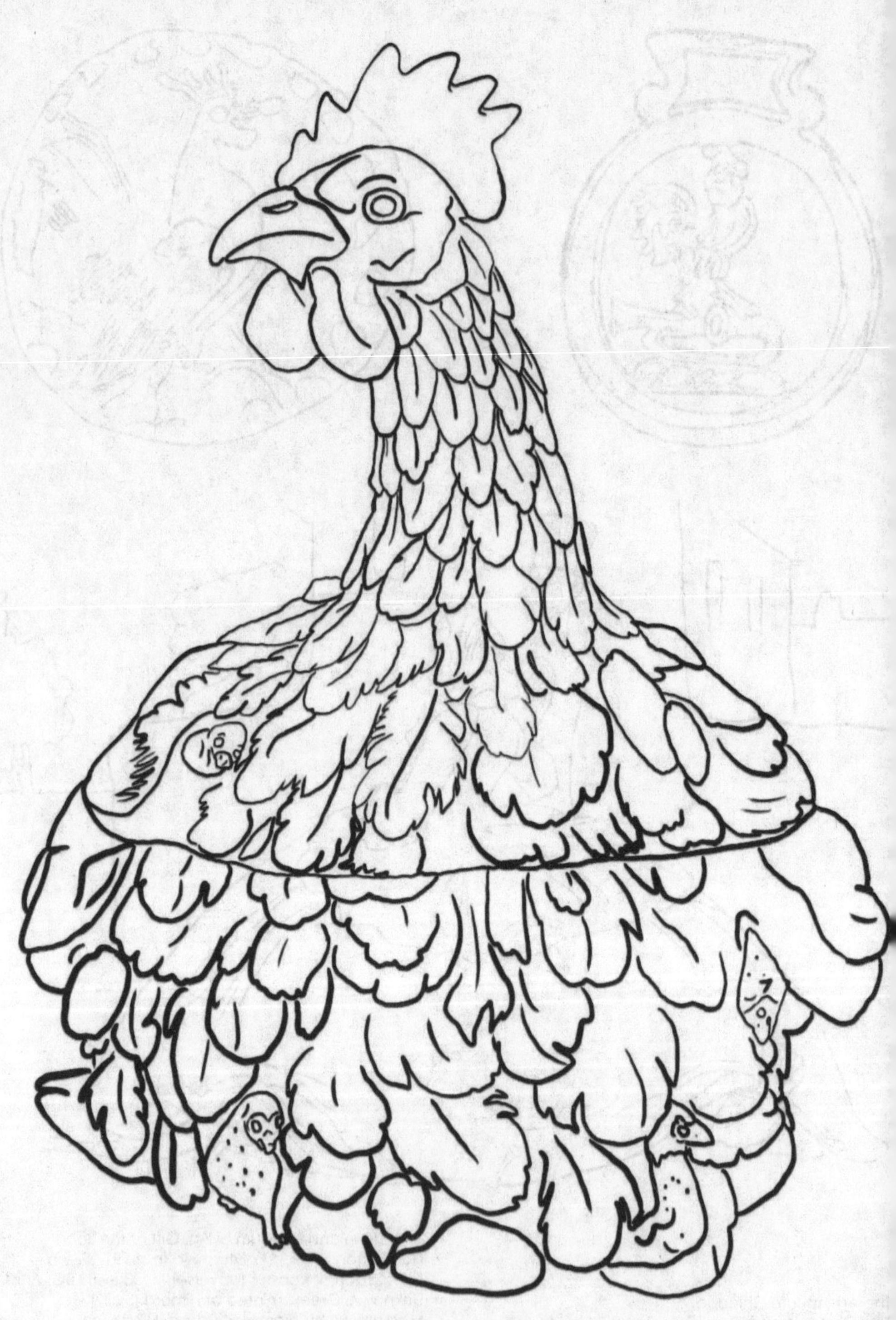

The Met Museum
Title: Tureen with Cover
Artist: Unknown, French, 1755
Medium: Tin-glazed earthenware

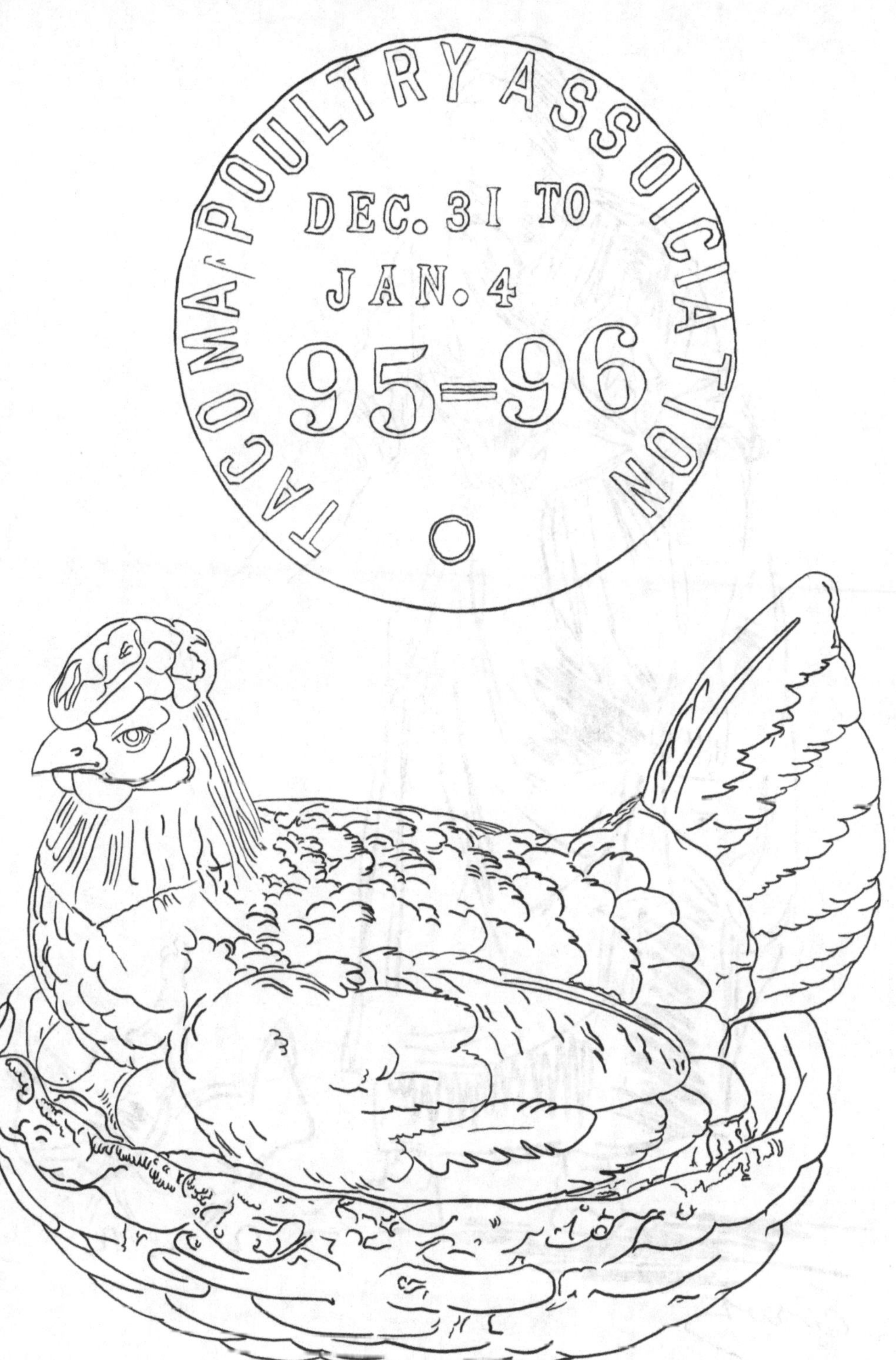

National Postal Museum, Smithsonian Institution
Title: Tacoma, Washington Owney Tag
Artist: Unknown
Medium: Metal
Depicted upper left

National Museum of Art
Title: Hen on Nest
Artist: Robert Gilson
Meduim: watercolor and graphite on paper
Depicted directly above

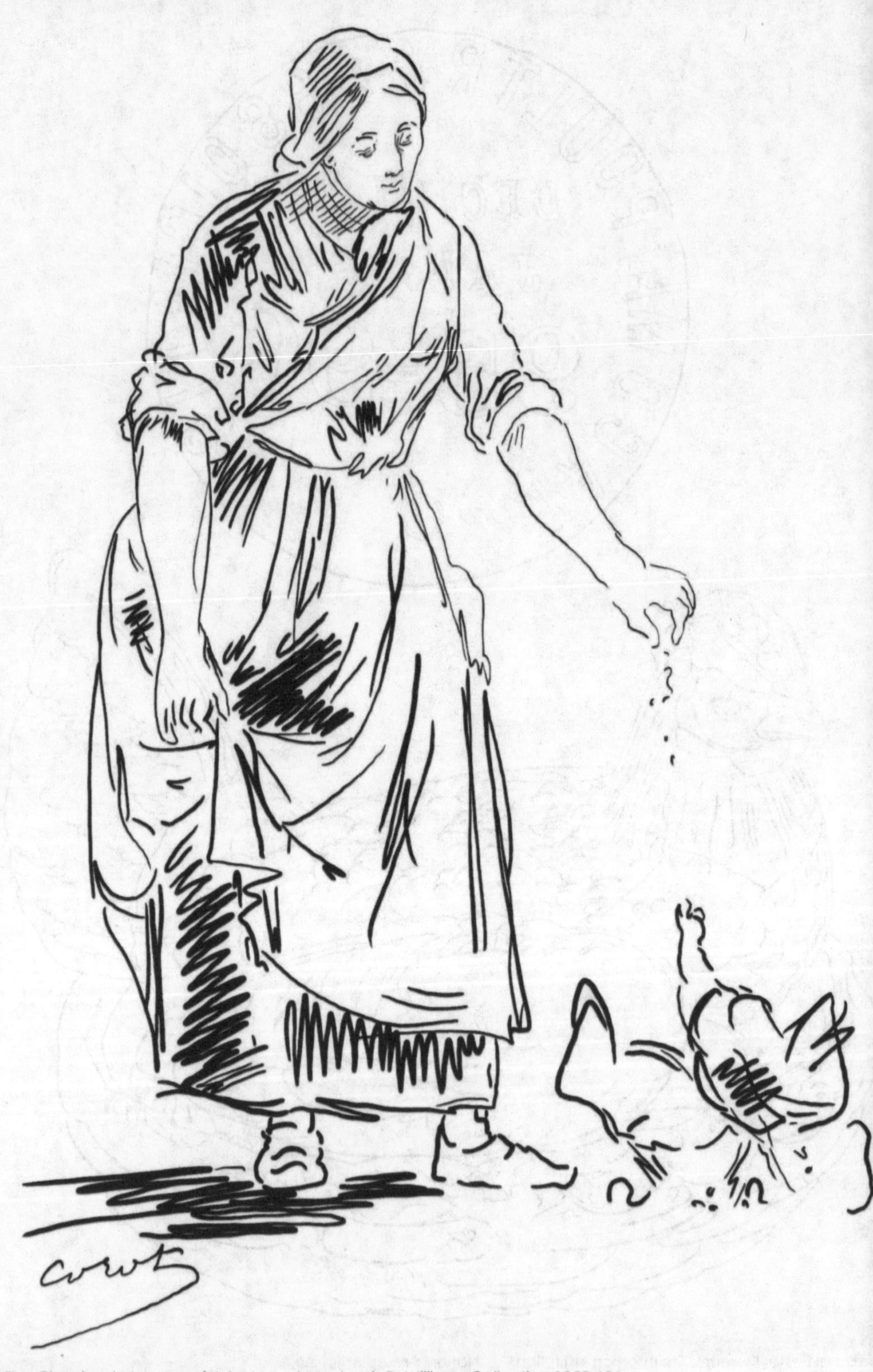

The Cleveland Museum of Art, Mr. and Mrs. Lewis B. Williams Collection 1955.654
Title: Peasant Girl Feeding Chickens, 1800s(?)
Artist: Jean Baptiste Camille Corot (French, 1796–1875)
Medium: Graphite; sheet: 29.3 x 19.7 cm (11 9/16 x 7 3/4 in.)

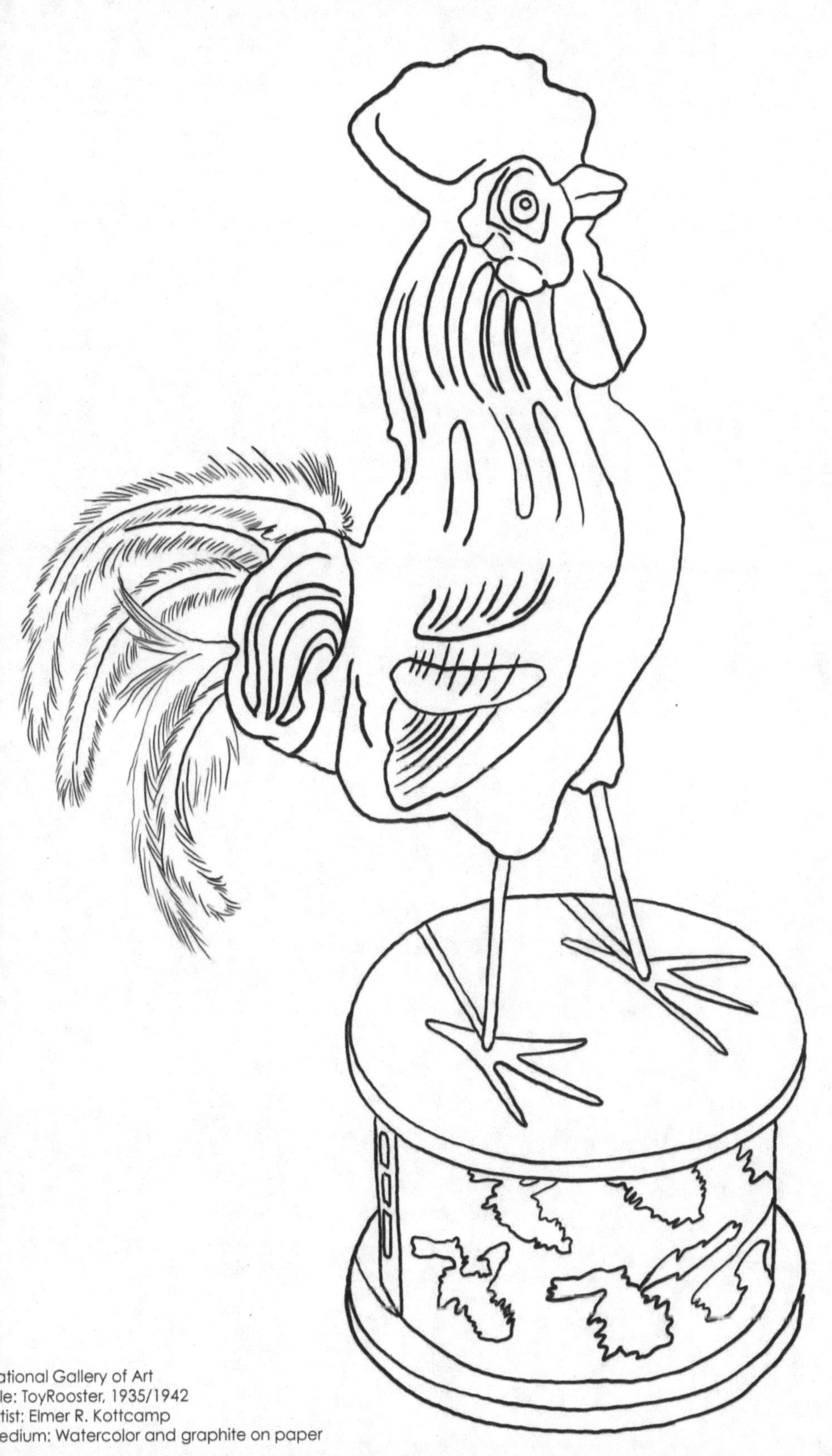

National Gallery of Art
Title: ToyRooster, 1935/1942
Artist: Elmer R. Kottcamp
Medium: Watercolor and graphite on paper

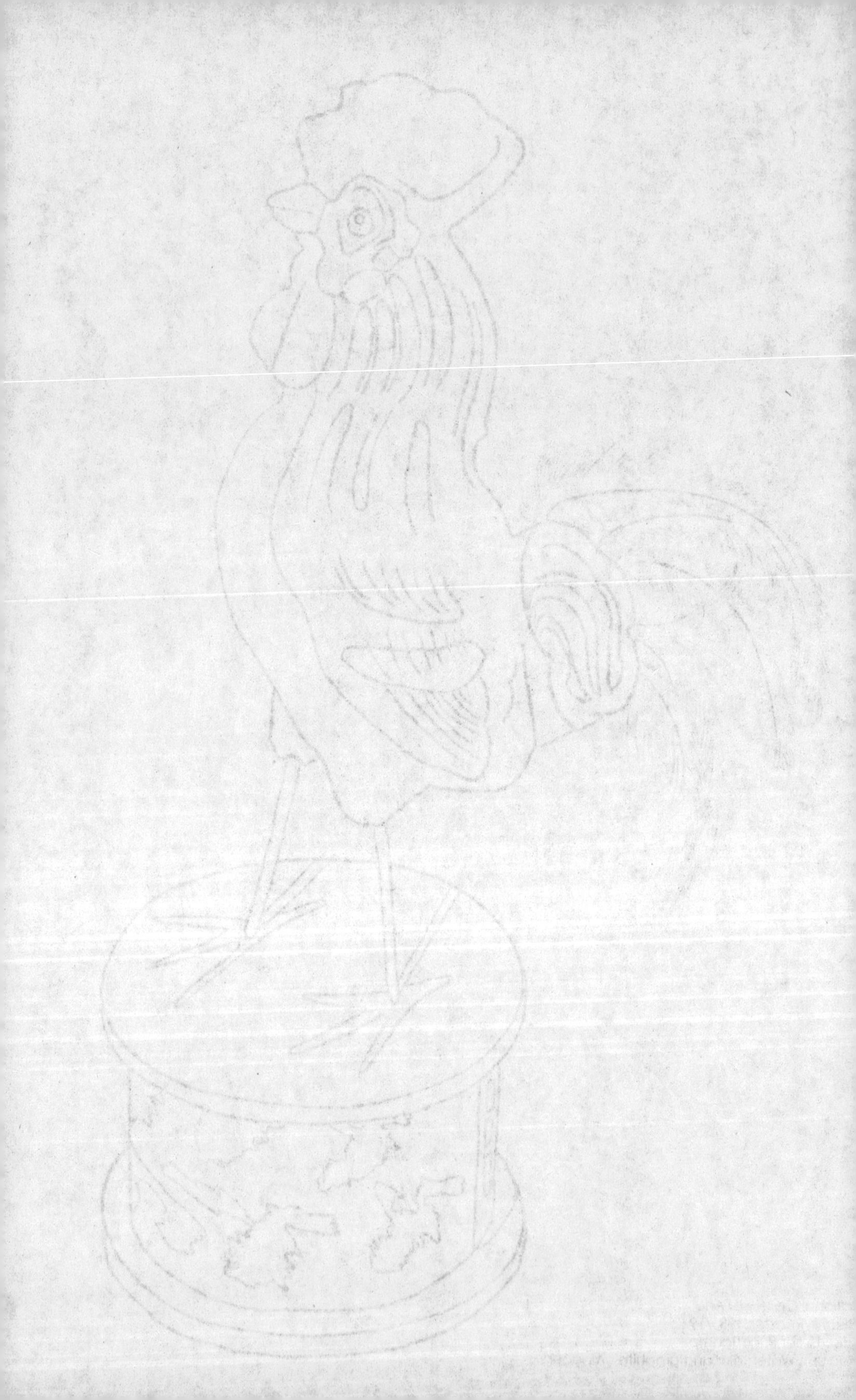